Giving Youth a Voice

Giving Youth a Voice
A Basis for Rethinking Adolescent Violence

Christie L. Barron

Fernwood Publishing • Halifax, Nova Scotia

Dedication

With love and thanks to my parents,
Herta Kukujuk Barron and F. Laurie Barron

Editing: Donna Davis
Design and production: Beverley Rach
Printed and bound in Canada by: Hignell Printing Limited

A publication of:
Fernwood Publishing
Box 9409, Station A
Halifax, Nova Scotia
B3K 5S3

Fernwood Publishing Company Limited gratefully acknowledges the financial support of the Ministry of Canadian Heritage and the Canada Council for the Arts for our publishing program.

Canadian Cataloguing in Publication Data

Barron, Christie.

    Giving youth a voice

    Includes bibliographical references.
    ISBN 1-55266-027-3

1. Juvenile delinquency.   2. Violence in adolescence.   I. Title.

HV9108.B37 2000   364.36   C00-950049-9

Contents

Chapter Four
The Youth Justice System
and Inherent Contradictions in Perception 90

Chapter Five
Conclusions: "Tainted Personalities" Mask Youths' Reality 119

Acknowledgements

There are several people without whom this project would not have been possible. The faculty, staff and students of the School of Criminology at Simon Fraser University played a significant role in the project. My sincere gratitude to Dr. Dany Lacombe, Dr. Robert Menzies, Christine, Deborah, Jane, Liz, Marie and Sharon. Prior to and during the interview process, I appreciated the assistance of Dr. Charles Singer, Dr. Dennis O'Toole, Don Hermanson, Bob Morris, Barb Kirland and the staff at Willingdon Detention Centre. I am especially grateful to the respondents whose willingness and insight made the research both valuable and enjoyable.

Thanks to the staff at Fernwood Publishing, particularly to Errol Sharpe for his enthusiasm and praise for the book from the outset.

My family also played an integral part in the completion of this project. My indebtedness to Mom and Dad for their support, newspaper clippings, feminist commentary, insightful suggestions and editing is beyond words. I am grateful to my brothers, Laurie and Scott, who support me in their own perverse way and who make me laugh. I give special thanks to my *oma*, Emma Kukujuk, and late *opa*, Wilhelm Kukujuk, who generously provided financial assistance during my graduate program. The support of my uncle, Roy Barron, is also greatly appreciated.

Lastly, I wish to express my thanks and love to Kelsey, whose faith in my ability to succeed is a constant source of strength.

Preface

Youth violence is one of the most talked about topics in contemporary society. It is difficult to consult a newspaper without finding a sensational account of youths attacking or even killing someone. The topic has become a favourite of the mass media because of its shock value and the opportunity it affords media to sensationalize and moralize. Indeed, youths and the crimes they commit have become symbolic of all that is wrong in society and have provoked a popular and academic discourse in which the very foundations of society are being questioned.

My interest in youth violence stems from my work as a master's degree student in the School of Criminology at Simon Fraser University. At the beginning of my graduate program I was intrigued by the attention commanded by the subject in both the press and the academy. I quickly uncovered a vast array of secondary literature detailing the causes, trends and strategies associated with youth violence. But what struck me in particular was the fact that the information available, whether in popular magazines, Corrections reports or professional discourse, was constructed from "expert" opinion. Conspicuously absent were the voices of young offenders themselves and their own experience-based ways of knowing. Evidently the perspectives of incarcerated youths have rarely been solicited and seldom respected in the formulation of knowledge about youth crime.

This book recognizes that youth testimony is a potentially important, yet untapped, source of understanding. In attempting to realize this potential, the study offers new insights into an age-old problem and embraces a unique approach to accessing the voices of young offenders. Hence, this study addresses the need for a re-appraisal of what is known about youth violence. And because it represents a departure from stand-ard approaches found in traditional disciplines, it also addresses meth-odological and theoretical issues. Like all scholarship that attempts to break away from the norm, this study questions the hegemony of traditional approaches to and understanding of youth violence.

Introduction

The initial interest in this study stemmed from media reports of recent incidents of youth violence which suggest that the public is concerned about the increase and severity of violence perpetrated by young people. While legal reforms are sought to treat violent young offenders as adults and to incarcerate them for longer periods, our government officials devote little effort to understanding youth violence itself. Academia has produced an extensive body of research on youth violence and delinquency (Bala et al. 1994; Corrado and Markwart 1994; Corrado et al. 1992; Doob et al. 1995; Acland 1995; Carrington 1995; Howell et al. 1995; Adler and Denmark 1995; Giroux 1996; James and Jenks 1996). It has investigated and continues to probe various factors, including biological, psychological, cultural and environmental dimensions, affecting youth violence. Yet this research tells us little about the way youths experience and interpret their own violence. How do they perceive their transgressions? How do they rationalize their actions? Do they take responsibility for their actions, or do they blame others? Moreover, there is little information on incarcerated youths and how they make sense of what is happening to them. This ignorance is a product of our general lack of faith in and a deep mistrust of children, particularly those capable of violence.

This book counters the lack of youth voice by comparing how young offenders understand and explain their reality to how recognized experts and official authorities assess the situation. Too often our attempts to make sense of youth violence rely exclusively on the reports and the perspectives of the latter authorities in the criminal justice system, such as probation officers and police, as well as those in academic circles, such as criminologists and psychologists. I will refer to both groups as "establishment authority," a term which encapsulates traditional approaches and is employed as a foil for the voices of children.

Although the Canadian Young Offenders Act (1984) deals with offenders from ages twelve through seventeen, I treat the distinction between the categories of "youth" and "child" as arbitrary. As Finch (1985) indicates, age, like gender, is based on biology, which tells us little about the social meaning and significance constructed around it. Youth is a general category which is given meaning only in specific circumstances and whose definition is subject to change (cited in James and Prout 1990:222). Acland (1995) also uses the term "youth" without a precise definition. He explains that "youth" is an empty signifier, "the age for which changes culturally, through time, across arenas, in different legal jurisdictions" (Acland 1995:20). The fact that "youth comes to mark different things … is an indication of its discursive constitution and of certain struggles waged in the process of its determination" (Acland 1995:21).

Thus, this book examines the extent to which and the ways in which there is a disjuncture between the perspectives of both youth offenders and establishment authorities on the issue of youth violence. This inquiry elicits valuable information on the basic understanding of violence by both groups; it probes the degree to which their perception is reaffirmed in society and in the youth justice system and it reveals how perceptions are formed and maintained. Realizing the conservative nature of the justice system leads to further inquiry into the possibilities of change.

The theoretical and methodological framework for this study is based on Dorothy Smith's *The Everyday World as Problematic: A Feminist Sociology* (1987). Smith's approach, described as "standpoint feminism," allows subjects a voice that reflects their perception and experience. Standpoint epistemology creates a space for those, such as youths, whose reality has been excluded from dominant discourse. The notion of "problematic" relates the inquiry to "the experience of members of a society as knowers located in actual lived situations in a new way" (Smith 1987:91). Of particular importance to this study is Smith's notion of the "ruling apparatus" (or relations of ruling) to which establishment authorities are integral. Examining how the privileged position of authorities informs both popular and "professional" discourse speaks to the current belief that the problem of violent offenders has reached a "crisis." Thus, the overall conceptual framework for this study utilizes several critical constructs which challenge conventional thought and methodology.

The data collection for the study involves interviews with thirty respondents: fifteen youths and fifteen establishment authorities. All but one youth, who was on probation, were incarcerated at the Willingdon Youth Detention Centre. Their demographics varied, as did their criminal records. All had been involved in violent crime, ranging from assault to murder. Establishment authorities included psychologists, psychiatrists, psychiatric social workers, the clinical director of Youth Court Services, police, probation officers, youth court judges, the local director of the new youth services team and the senior correctional officer in charge of programs (OCP) at Willingdon. Interviews were semi-structured and involved open-ended questions about the respondents' experiences in the youth justice system, their family and peer relations, their explanations of violent behaviour and those deemed responsible, and their understanding of punishment and the treatment of violent offenders. The impact of official knowledge and relations of ruling, which affect both youths and the establishment authority, is exposed through a comparative analysis of their respective standpoints. In addition, a comparison between the youths' testimony and the institutional files recorded by establishment authorities further determines a difference in perception. While maintaining the integrity of my respondents' voices, the data evoke analysis from both a critical and social constructionist perspective. The knowledge informing the discourse on violent youth offenders does not reflect any form of truism but is created and manipulated to serve wider functions (Acland 1995; Foucault 1979; Giroux 1996; Kelly 1992; Schissel 1997).

There is a severe disjuncture in the perceptions of youths and establishment authorities on youth violence, and this disjuncture holds important implications. Not only is the voice of youths counter hegemonic to the justice system overall; it also fills information gaps in academic and, more specifically, criminological literature.

In addition to correcting public perception, this proactive study may benefit youths themselves. We must fully understand the experience of youth before we can know what they need in treatment. Being cognizant of their everyday lives and the way they perceive their actions, particularly in comparison to how others interpret their behaviour, will illuminate a topic that presently commands national attention.

Chapter One

Defining the Parameters
of Youth Violence

"A lull before the teenage storm: Teen violence stats are up and more crime is on the way" … warnings of a "coming youth time bomb." (*Western Report* August 19, 1996: 12, 24)

"…we're running for cover," remarked the parent of a witness to the 7-Eleven beating … "If we go to the police, these guys will come after us and our homes." (Brunet 1996:42)

The issue of youth violence has produced fear in society according to popular discourse. The anxiety over the supposed "youth crisis" is manifest in a plethora of newspaper accounts, magazine articles and media reports. The descriptions may reflect a moral panic in society fed by the media or there may in fact be a significant problem with the number of violent acts committed by young people. Most likely, the reality involves a combination of the two. The extent to which these interpretations are true is made problematic by the fact that, although academia has produced extensive research on youth violence and delinquency, the findings are inconclusive and based on incomplete, if not faulty, methodology. Although the problems of traditional, positivist studies have been brought to light by social constructionist explanations in the form of cultural studies (Acland 1995; Giroux 1996), even these do not present a complete picture of youth violence. The purpose of this chapter is to examine existing literature on the supposed "youth crisis" and to illustrate how it is constructed and challenged, indicating the need for an alternative approach in understanding youth violence.

Trends and Statistics

In examining youth violence there is a need to determine if official statistics validate public fear over the supposed increase in violence. Current "common sense" accepts that something has gone wrong with today's youth, reflected, for example, in an article indicating a 467 percent increase in the murder arrest rate for eighteen-year-olds (*Western Report*

1996:11). What is not clear, however, is whether the crisis of violence is more in the perception than the reality. The degree of violence in Canada differs from that in the U.S.; nevertheless, in both countries official statistics remain a source of unresolved debate. Clearly, problems with the accuracy of statistics can produce distortions in perception.

Official statistics on crime in Canada indicate an increase both in the number of youth (ages 12–17) charged with violent criminal offences and in violence-related youth court cases. According to the Revised Uniform Crime Reporting (UCR) Survey, of the 135,348 youth indicted with Criminal Code offences in 1992, 15 percent were charged with violent crimes, a 10.5 percent increase from 1986 (Statistics Canada 1994, cited in Bala et al. 1994:7). In addition, of the 115,000 cases heard in youth court, 19 percent had a violent offence as the principal charge, representing a 9 percent increase (Leonard 1993). According to Corrado and Markwart, between 1986 and 1992 the per capita rate of young persons charged with Criminal Code offences increased by 25 percent (1994:350), mirroring "a real and substantial increase in youth violence in Canada in recent years" (1994:354).

Carrington (1995) challenges the findings of Corrado and Markwart. He claims an increase in the number of young persons charged does not necessarily indicate an increase in actual youth crime; rather, it represents changes in the identification of young offenders by police and in the propensity of police to lay charges, which increased during the 1980s (Carrington 1995:62). Carrington argues that a better indicator would be the police-reported rate of youth crime. However, the Canadian Centre for Justice Statistics claims that the reliability of "youths not charged" data is unknown and that these statistics may not have been uniformly collected (Kingsley 1994:15). Corrado and Markwart have reiterated that, whichever indicator is used, there is still an evident increase in youth violence based on a statistical appraisal of Criminal Code offences (1995:75). In addition, there is disagreement as to the most appropriate time period in considering pre- and post-Young Offenders Act data and the "modest impacts of the minimum age, the enormous effects of the uniform maximum age, changes in procedure and evidentiary requirements and changes in the definition of offences" (Corrado and Markwart 1994:77).

There is further debate over whether categories of the Criminal Code are a reliable guide to discerning the degree of violence. Carrington (1995) argues that not all offences classified as "against the person" constitute violence. For example, assault is defined in Section 256 of the Criminal Code as "touching without the consent of the complainant" (Greenspan 1994:445). Carrington explains that "such touching—or attempting or threatening to touch—may, particularly if it is sexual, have serious consequences and be the object of serious social disapprobation" (1995:67). He claims, however, that it is inaccurate to refer to Level 1[1] physical and sexual assaults as violent, a position which is described by both Corrado and Markwart (1994) and Roberts (1995) as erroneous and insulting to victims. They explain that Level 1 common assault is a hybrid offence that includes a wide range of behaviours. In fact, 83 percent of victims of Level 1 assault suffered a physical injury, not to mention the psychological harm resulting from sexual assault (Corrado and Markwart 1994:81; Roberts 1995:90–91). Moreover, the definition of sexual assault was reformed in 1983 to reflect the violent, as opposed to sexual, nature of these offences (Stuart 1993).

While still disagreeing with Carrington, Corrado and Markwart (1994) comment that, despite the large percentage increases in violent youth crime, the number of serious cases in Canada remains small both historically and in relation to youth crime statistics for the United States. Therefore the increase should not form the premise for Draconian control-oriented reforms:

> These cases, again, are few in number and great care must be taken to ensure that any proposals for reform do not become simplistic, over-reaching, and, in the end, self-defeating, a scenario that appears to be unfolding in the U.S. (Corrado and Markwart 1994:84)

Statistics on violent crime in the United States in 1993 indicate that juveniles committed 13 percent of all violent crimes (as measured by crimes cleared by arrest) (Howell et al. 1995:1) and that the rate of violent crime by youth (10-17 years of age) increased more than 25 percent in the last decade. Moreover, the rate was up for youth from all races, social classes and lifestyles (Chisholm 1995:47). Between 1988 and 1992 juvenile violent crime arrests increased 47 percent with murder rising 51 percent. The leading cause of death among African Americans aged 15-19 is homicide (Acland 1995:7). Thus, according to several authors, the "seriousness of the problem is supported by national statistics on youth violence" (Lattimore et al. 1995:55).

As in Canada, statistics on youth violence in the United States are debatable. Acland (1995) argues that the perception that youth violence is more serious today than in the past is based on "taken-for-granted" measures of crisis. For example, according to a congressional report on adolescent health, the levels of violence are still far below those of the mid-1970s (U.S. Congress 1991:591 cited in Acland 1995:8). Although the authors of this report cite an increase in murder and non-negligent manslaughter committed by those between thirteen and eighteen years of age, they also point out that the majority of young offenders commit minor offences, leaving a very small subset who commit multiple, serious offences (1991:594–96), which is consistent with literature tracing back for more than a generation. Furthermore, although the increases appear significant, reported arrest rate statistics may exaggerate the youth violence problem because they do not indicate the actual number of violent crimes committed by youth (Howell et al. 1995:2). Rather, arrest statistics are a reflection of policing practice. Also, the tendency for youth to commit violent crime in groups creates differences between arrest and clearance rates, which in turn distort the FBI arrest statistics. An examination of statistics on violent youth crime is important because, in addition to outlining "official understanding" of youth violence, it underscores the need for an alternative approach to the subject. A quantitative account lends insight into the debate over the extent of youth violence and illustrates the considerable confusion in the area. In fact, it appears impossible to use statistics to grasp the extent of youth violence. The polemical nature of the literature on crime statistics indicates a lack of agreement in the professional ranks, which undoubtedly contributes to public misconceptions. Much of this confusion stems from methodological issues, the most obvious being that scholars do not even agree on what constitutes youth violence itself.

In any debate over the increase or decrease in crime, the social construction of statistics must be recognized. In 1962, Canada joined much of the industrialized world in adopting the Uniform Crime Reporting (UCR) procedure to standardize reporting across jurisdictions and police forces (Palys 1995:379). Therefore, when crime statistics are released they are frequently perceived as "objective" indicators of crime rather than the end result of a human process. As Palys correctly emphasizes, "every statistic, regardless of whether it is the crime index published by Statistics Canada or a self-report to a survey, is in some sense a social construction, and it comes into being as a function of various psychological, sociological and organizational processes" (1995:379). Thus, as Schissel contends, "it is important to reiterate that youth crime rates are largely a function of the structure and nature of legal practice and not of increases or decreases in actual crimes committed" (1997:99).

A cultural studies analysis offers an alternative view of statistics on youth crime and recognizes the problems of traditional approaches. As illustrated in the debates over crime statistics, the empirical validity of the measures can be debated at a number of different levels. Acland recognizes in his book, *Youth, Murder, Spectacle: The Cultural Politics of "Youth in Crisis,"* that arguments are presented to interpret the findings, "which suggests that conclusions are provisional and to various degrees are sites of contestation" (1995:5). He explains that questioning how accurate the criminological measures are reveals only part of the picture. What is of utmost importance is how the findings are deployed.

> [While a criminological report] provides a description of a social phenomenon, it also tells of the attention paid to that phenomenon, or rather to that set of measures and judgements that purport to indicate the existence of a crisis. Whether or not the situation is historically unique, it is certainly being taken as such. (Acland 1995:5)

Although Acland's critique provides a much needed account of the social construction of statistics and the classification of "youth in crisis," it does not go far enough in addressing the perspective of the offenders themselves. The official word on the extent of violence is monopolized and disseminated by experts in the field with little consideration for self-reported data by violent youth. Moreover, the few studies that do incorporate such self-reported data (Cornell and Gelles 1982; Sugarman and Hotaling 1991; Fairholm 1993) often use the information for numerical purposes without providing the perceptions of youth in their own words. Clearly, there is a need to broaden our knowledge of youth violence through an approach that allows youth to contribute their insights.

Definitions of Youth Violence

It is evident in the literature that neither the extent nor the nature of youth violence is well understood due to questions of meaning and interpretation. "Definitions of youth violence vary widely depending on the person, profession, or agency defining it" (Bala et al. 1994:6). On the one hand, explain Bala and his co-authors, youth-serving organizations such as schools tend to include a variety of behaviours and circumstances in their definitions. For example, Ontario's Wellington County School Board argues:

> [A] violent activity is characterized by verbal or written threats; physical, emotional, sexual abuse or harassment; or racial harassment by an individual or group of individuals which has the effect of impairing or might have the effect of impairing the health and welfare of any student or staff member. (MacDougall 1993 cited in Bala et al. 1994:6)

On the other hand, they note that the Criminal Code provides a narrower definition of violence. Under Section 256(1)(a), for instance, an assault is defined as the intentional application of force without consent. Furthermore, though a "consensual" fight between two students in a school yard would not be considered a criminal offence unless someone was seriously harmed and/or weapons were involved, it would be defined as youth violence by the school board.

The American Psychological Association states in the article "Violence and Youth: Psychology's Response" that "violence is not a random, unaccountable or inevitable occurrence … [m]any factors, both individual and social, contribute to an individual's propensity to use violence, and many of these factors are within our power to change" (cited in Bala et al. 1994:5). Clinical psychologist June Chisholm borrows an operational definition of violence which emphasizes

> a uniting of the self in action.… [Violence] is an organizing of one's powers to prove one's power, to establish the worth of the self. It is risking all, a committing all, an asserting all. But it unites the different elements in the self, omitting rationality. Whatever its motive or its consequences may be within the violent person, its result is generally destructive to the others in the situation. (May 1972:188 cited in Chisholm 1995:48)

The Public Health Service of the U.S. Department of Health and Human Services (1991) claims that violence is being defined increasingly as a public health problem in America because it poses a serious threat to the health and well-being of millions of Americans (cited in Howell et al. 1995:23). In his study of individuals who cannot restrain themselves from inflicting injury, Lefer (1984) creates an obscure classification system of the "violence-prone individual" (VPI). He explains that, depending on the strength of repression, suppression, inhibition, reaction formation, rationalization and conscience, a VPI may be categorized as: one who uses violence as a means to an end without a need for justification (for example, a "sociopath" involved in organized crime); one who uses violence as a means to an end but must justify it to his or her conscience; one who is violent only in a dissociated or drugged state; or one who becomes symbiotic with another VPI and aids the other in committing violence (cited in Chisholm 1995:49).

In addition to its various definitions, violence is usually described by action or type. The most common types of violent youth behaviour include assaults (causing bodily harm); weapons offences; robbery; harassment; intimidation and extortion; homicide; sexual offences; and prostitution (Bala et al. 1994:41). This behaviour is manifest in six main areas of concern. The first type is school violence, represented in a variety of behaviours ranging from the traditional "school bully" to group violence and intimidation of students and staff. Bullies are described as adolescent males who have experienced dysfunctional personal, social and familial development and whose parents have used excessive physical punishment (Weiler and Associates 1994:27–28 cited in Bala et al. 1994:96).

In more severe cases, youth gangs move into schools to recruit participants for thefts, assaults and drug dealing. Here again it is difficult to present an accurate picture of gang involvement because of the various perceptions of what constitutes a "gang." Some describe groups of anti-social people who "hang out" at shopping malls as gangs; others reserve the term for hard-core, organized crime rings (Bala et al. 1994:116). Independent of formal definitions, incidents of victimization at school are more frequent than currently believed, considering that an estimated 80 percent of cases go unreported (Bala et al. 1994:94).

The Survey of Student Life was conducted by Artz and Riecken (1994) "to provide profiles of students who report that they engage in violence at schools" (Artz 1998:26). Artz states that their initial task was to define a "violent" person and then to differentiate between violent and non-violent youth. They used a 1991 questionnaire developed by Barnes, a Canadian researcher in the fields of family violence, addictions and substance abuse, which apparently "meant that we were working with a measure that had been previously tested and that lent credibility to our findings" (Artz 1998:27).

> Of the 13 variables investigated, the one that spoke most directly to violence reads, "during the past year, how often have you beaten up another kid," thus defining violence as "beating up another kid."… For the purposes of analysis, students' answers were dichotomized into "never," and "once or more." These groups were termed "nonhitters" and "hitters," respectively. This dichotomy was deemed to represent the clearest and most natural distinction between the two groups, and was used for both males and females in the creation of the profiles of the protagonists. (Artz 1998:27)

The second type of youth violence is collective violence. The most common form of collective violence in Canada occurs within informal groups of friends, as opposed to organized gangs, who become involved spontaneously. The actions are motivated by attempts to protect friends; by competition over boyfriends/girlfriends; and by hatred for others based on their gender, ethnicity, sexual orientation or disability (Bala et al. 1994:115). Youths involved in informal groups come from diverse backgrounds. They include the stereotypical "at-risk" youths who have social, personal and family problems and who are often immigrants and refugees experiencing difficulty integrating into educational, social and employment situations. They may be "wannabes," mimicking gang behaviour to gain status, material possessions or s sense of belonging. Violent group behaviour may also be the result of boredom or a search for thrills (Acland 1995:6–7).

The third type of youth violence is directed at siblings, parents and other caregivers in the family and in similar residential settings. Family dysfunction, limited options to leave home, a lack of respect for authority and differing social and cultural expectations contribute to sibling and parent abuse (Bala et al. 1994:135). Because violence between siblings is so common, incidents are rarely seen as manifestations of youth violence; however, a recent pre-test by Ellis and DeKeseredy (1994) indicates that 66 percent of siblings in Canada engage in physical and verbal/emotional violence (cited in Bala et al. 1994:137). In addition, 5 percent to 12 percent of adolescents report kicking, punching, biting, beating up and using or threatening to use a knife or gun on their parents (Cornell and Gelles 1982 cited in Bala et al. 1994:137). The rates of sibling or parent abuse are related both to the frequency of other forms of family violence in the home and to the family authority structure. Violence directed at others in alternative residential settings and treatment facilities is also gaining the attention of correctional, mental health and child welfare officials as well as police (Bala et al. 1994:135). Some professionals suggest that increased frequency and intensity in this type of youth violence may be caused by a shortage of programs, staff and training. In addition, there is the negative influence of mixing high-risk violent-prone youth with non-violent youth in group homes.

The fourth type of youth violence is dating violence. According to Health Canada's National Clearinghouse on Family Violence, dating violence is recognized as the emotional, physical and/or sexual abuse of one partner by the other in a dating relationship where the couple is not living together (Phaneuf 1990). Males attribute their violent behaviour to jealousy over a real or perceived third party; alcohol and substance use; and anger over being denied sexual intercourse. Females cite uncontrollable anger; self-defence; jealousy; and retaliation as the principal reasons for engaging in violence with their dating partner (Sugarman and Hotaling 1991; Fairholm 1993). Though any abused partner is at risk of becoming abusive her/himself later on, males are more likely to initiate violence than females (Bergman 1992; Fitzpatrick and Halliday 1992; DeKeseredy and Kelly 1993). This reflects the fact that violence in general is disproportionately a male phenomenon.

Sexual assault is the fifth type of youth violence. Research indicates that sexual offences committed by youth may be more violent and more intrusive than those perpetrated by adults (Hornick et al. 1994 cited in Bala et al. 1994:169). Sexually assaultive youths typically have family problems of physical and/or sexual abuse as well as a high degree of parental substance abuse and mental illness (Awad et al. 1984; Pierce and Pierce 1987; Bagley and Shewchuk-Dann 1991 cited in Bala et al. 1994:171). The youths themselves often have learning impediments and behaviour problems. Offender profiles also reveal that a substantial number of young males and females who engage in abusive sexual behaviour are under the age of twelve years (Hornick et al. 1994 cited in Bala et al. 1994:170).

Violent behaviour in children under twelve, the sixth type of youth violence, concerns a group that is classified differently from the "youth" recognized in the Young Offenders Act. The most common violent offence committed by children is assault, which constitutes 5 percent of all offences (Statistics Canada 1994 cited in Bala et al. 1994:189). Children also committed 10 percent of all sexual offences involving those eighteen years of age and under; these offences are described as "very intrusive" (Hornick et al. 1994 cited in Bala et al. 1994:189). For many youths, patterns of criminal behaviour are evident in childhood. Symptoms may include hyperactivity; limited attention; poor learning skills; and assorted anti-social behaviour as a result of inconsistent and uncaring parenting, social and economic deprivation, poor nutrition and health care, family violence and other barriers to normal development (American Psychological Association 1993 cited in Bala et al. 1994:189). For this reason, early intervention and prevention through appropriate social, psychological and educational services are crucial.

Weaknesses in existing studies on youth violence stem from reporting and accuracy problems due to the discretion in definitions and lack of published material in certain areas. Few studies have examined the concept of youth violence beyond behaviours that are reported as criminal incidents (Bala et al. 1994:5). For example, two national consultations (Weiler and Associates Ltd. 1994; Walker 1993) claim to provide definitional "insight," but no precise definition of youth violence is given. Rather, these studies simply perpetuate current alleged trends in youth violence: younger perpetrators; an increased female participation and use of weapons; and more intense, random and vicious acts of violence (Bala et al. 1994:8). It is interesting to note that only "professionals" were interviewed during the consultations, limiting understanding of the problem to expert opinion. Moreover, discussion of each of the six types of violence included a description of the "offender profile," with no consideration given to the self-perception of the offender. The explanations used to make sense of and classify youth violence often fail to recognize the effect of cultural and social factors.

In his cultural studies approach, Giroux (1996) provides more detail regarding the social circumstance surrounding violent youth. He claims that youth most likely to be involved in violent crime are part of what he describes as a "fugitive culture." This term "designates … a conflicting and dynamic set of experiences rooted in a working-class youth culture marked by flows and uncertain interventions into daily life" (Giroux 1996:8). He explains that currently the crisis of youth is represented through the imagery and discourse of popular culture, which contains increasing symbolic, material and institutional violence. Fugitive cultures are represented in malls, rock music, gangsta rap and urban basketball courts, while youth, as a self- and social construction, has become in the public eye indeterminate, alien and sometimes hazardous. "Youth cultures are often viewed in the popular press as aberrant, unpredictable, and dangerous in terms of the investments they produce, social regulations they affirm, and the anti-politics they sometimes legitimate" (Giroux 1996:11).

To an extent Giroux's explanation echoes the "moral panic" literature common in the critical criminological research of the late 1960s and 1970s. This literature focused on how rare events at certain times conjured collective hostility and ultimately a public demand for law reform. It also "concentrated on how official and popular culture accounts of criminality were based on overgeneralized, inaccurate and stereotypical descriptions of criminals and their associations and how the public panics that resulted were mostly directed at working-class or marginalized [youths]" (Schissel 1997:12).

Stanley Cohen (1980) developed the concept of "moral panic" to understand the attack on youth in Britain in the 1960s. The construction of the "Mods and Rockers" illustrates how the concept of moral panic is based on social stereotypes of unruly youth. Cohen (1980) coined the term "folk devils" to identify those outgroups, such as violent youth, who are perceived as a threat to the moral and social being of society. Folk devils are created and imbued with characteristics that set them apart from normal law-abiding citizens. Often such characteristics are inaccurate. For example, although youths are often depicted in the media as inherently evil, their crimes, according to Snyder and Sickmund (1995), are transitory and involve very little harm (cited in Schissel 1997:31).

As Schissel recognizes, "equally important as his critical analysis of the media and political motives, however, was Cohen's specification of the connection between the particular moral panic and the social, political and economic atmosphere of 1960s England" (Schissel 1997:13). Hall et al. (1978) incorporated a Marxist interpretation in their understanding of moral panics by indicating that they serve an elitist purpose. "The work of Hall and his co-authors is particularly important and instructive in that it studies the connections between ideological production, the mass media and those in positions of power" (Schissel 1997:13). In his book, *Blaming Children: Youth Crime, Moral Panic and the Politics of Hate*, Schissel (1997:10) expands on these earlier works to explain the current fear and hatred of children in society through "a discussion of the role of media and its affiliations with information/political systems, with its readers and viewers and with corporate Canada."

Although Acland (1995), Giroux (1996) and Schissel (1997) contextualize how we (mis)understand youth, any precise definition of youth violence will be incomplete without incorporating the understanding of those to whom the definition applies. Otherwise, our definition will be one-dimensional and one-sided, confined to adults and unmindful of what youths themselves can contribute to our prescriptive understanding. We must actively consider the standpoint of youth to present a more accurate definition of youth violence.

Contributing Factors

At issue in the social response to youth crime are the several factors deemed by establishment authority to contribute to violent behaviour. The literature offers as many "causes" for violence as there are cases of violent incidents. As Adler and Denmark (1995) explain, causes are often multifaceted and uncertain, making them difficult to clearly measure and identify.

Overall, there is a clear division in the literature analyzing the nature of violent crime. Those on one side of the debate view violent crime as a product of larger structural inequities and social systems and advocate a restorative approach that respects the needs of youths. Those on the other side point to individual responsibility, personality and pathology and demand a punitive response. Jacqueline Barkley (1998), in her article addressing the commodification of parenting in relation to the youth crisis, argues that the analysis must be balanced between these two seemingly dichotomous perspectives.

> We need to understand the socioeconomic causes of [the youths'] antisocial behaviour and relocate that behaviour in a place where we can simultaneously acknowledge the victim experience of children and their role as perpetrators. We must not surrender the question of morality and private behaviour to those whose perspective on it is hierarchical, patriarchal, or authoritarian. (Barkley 1998:319–20)

In essence, contributing factors of youth violence are often framed as being in favour of either social justice or personal morality.

One explanation for the increase in violence among youth is the availability and use of firearms. A 1990 American survey found that one in twenty-five high school students carried a gun at least once during a thirty-day period (Chisholm 1995:47). In New York City, arrests on gun charges for children aged 7–15 increased 75 percent between 1987 and 1990 (*New York Times* 1992 cited in Chisholm 1995). Furthermore, firearms kill more than 10 percent of people who die before the age of twenty (Acland 1995:7), and in 1992 more than 85 percent of murder victims aged 15–19 were killed with firearms (Howell et al. 1995:5). The availability of handguns increases the risk of homicide in urban areas among all age groups (Sloan et al. 1990 cited in Howell et al. 1995:6) and is associated with higher levels of violence in the home (Saltzman et al. 1992 cited in Howell et al. 1995:6). Moreover, Wolman (1995:xvii) argues that the problems stemming from easy access to abundant lethal weapons are compounded by the weakness of police and courts in dealing with this issue, thus contributing to the increase in youth violence.

The National Academy of Sciences Panel on High-Risk Youth also identified several factors that contribute to an increase in youth violence. The decline in income levels of families with young children and the associated problems of growing up in poverty greatly contribute to offending behaviour. Poverty often leads to physical and mental health problems, low academic achievement, unemployment, delinquency and exposure to socially disorganized neighbourhoods, which provide little opportunity for legitimate success (Howell et al. 1995:9). Involvement with delinquent peers, which often includes gang participation, is also related to violence among youth (Lattimore et al. 1995:58).

And what about the harm caused by early victimization? Howell et al. claim that one of the most neglected topics in current debates about violent crime is the victimization of youth. There were 2.7 million incidents of child abuse and neglect reported to U.S. authorities in 1991, and an estimated 500,000 children run away from home each year (Howell et al. 1995:10). It is evident that youths who experience and witness abuse are more likely to become perpetrators of crime, violence and abuse (Finkelhor and Dziuba-Leatherman 1994; Hotaling et al. 1989; Kruttschnitt and Dornfeld 1991; Lewis et al. 1989; Widom 1992; Smith and Thornberry 1993 cited in Howell et al. 1995:31). Extensive use of drugs and alcohol is also linked to violent offences by both youths and adults (Lattimore et al. 1995:58). Numerous studies currently argue that youths victimized by alcohol before birth and who now suffer from fetal alcohol syndrome (FAS) are also susceptible to violent behaviour. It is interesting to note how the field of medicine has become a means of explanation. The victimization cause is now medicalized and psycholo-gized.

There are additional psychological explanations for violence. Abused children tend to be more aggressive and to exhibit more psychopathology than their peers (Aber and Cicchetti 1984). In his clinical studies, Green (1985) identified other factors, such as identification with the aggressor or victim embedded in the compulsive re-enactment of early traumatic events; paranoid distortion of object relationships; fears of object loss; and central nervous system impairment (cited in Chisholm 1995:51).

Several of these variables also contribute to recidivism among violent youth. An American study of 1949 individuals paroled by the California Youth Authority indicates that re-arrest is significantly influenced by prior arrests for violence and family pathology variables, including family violence and parental criminality (Lattimore et al. 1995:54). Vio-lent offending by youth is also part of a repertoire of lawlessness that includes property offences, drug dealing and other miscellaneous crimes; violence is more likely to occur as arrests accumulate. However, Haapanen (1991) found that although violent and non-violent criminality are re-lated, violence is not simply a by-product of general offending (cited in Lattimore et al. 1995:55). A history of previous aggression and violence is the best predictor. Institutional behaviour that includes threats or aggres-sion is strongly associated with the risk of re-arrest for violence (Lattimore et al. 1995:75). This reiterates a common belief that, because recidivism stems from the individual, once a delinquent, always a delinquent.

The traditional search for "causes" of youth violence continues to focus on individual factors. The difficulty in measurement and identifi-cation reflects the failure of positivistic approaches to recognize that "causes" are social constructions that are culture- and time-specific. A partial remedy to this ignorance is found in cultural studies explanations.

A more recent explanation, and passionately debated issue, is the powerful influence of media on youth violence (American Psychological Association 1993; Centerwall 1992). Some argue that aggression and violence have become idealized in American television, film, video and other media. It is estimated that the average American views seven hours of television a day, during which time the major broadcast networks average five acts of violence an hour. For the last fifteen years, networks have averaged about twenty-five acts of violence an hour on Saturday morning television (Giroux 1996:60). Furthermore, researchers estimate that children will watch 100,000 acts of simulated violence before gradu-ating from elementary school and will have viewed 18,000 murders on T.V. by the age of eighteen (Giroux 1996:60). Incidents of violence in the media are so commonplace that they define our experience of everyday life and appear to diminish our compassion for real suffering (Giroux

1996:65). Although his study may be methodologically questionable, Centerwall (1992) estimates that if television had not developed to the extent that it has, there would be 10,000 fewer homicides, 70,000 fewer rapes, and 700,000 fewer injurious assaults each year in the U.S. (cited in Howell et al. 1995:9).

Seemingly, media have become a substitute for experience "and what constitutes understanding is grounded in a decentered and diasporic world of difference, displacement, and negation" (Giroux 1996:33). Giroux cites five current films as examples of how postmodern youth are uniquely alien, strange and disconnected from the real world. In these films, youths view death as a mere spectacle, a matter of form rather than substance (Giroux 1996:35). He explains one scenario in director Tim Hunter's film *River's Edge* (1986):

> Life imitates art when committing murder and getting stoned are given equal moral weight in the formula of the Hollywood spectacle, a spectacle which in the end flattens the complex representations of youth while constructing their identities through ample servings of pleasure, violence, and indifference. (Giroux 1996:35)

The effect of these images is damaging. Wolman claims that "[t]he present social climate of excessive hedonism, with its widespread 'have fun' attitudes encourages alcoholism and drug abuse and the 'do whatever pleases you' mentality ... [and that] this selfish social climate fosters sociopathic personality" (1995:xvi).

As Giroux explains, missing from the media is any critical commentary on the relationship between the spread of the culture of violence and the representations of violence that saturate the mass media (1996:28). Media fail to address the social conditions that produce a generation of young people enveloped in despair, violence, crime, poverty and racism. Giroux calls for a reversal of the "mean-spirited" discourse of the 1980s and 1990s, during which mainly Black victims in the U.S. were blamed for myriad social problems (1996:30). In fact, much of Giroux's book focuses on the portrayal of violent Black-on-Black fratricide.

> Such racially coded discourse serves to mobilize White fears and legitimate drastic measures in social policy in the name of crime reform.... [M]oreover, the discourse of race and violence provides a sense of social distance and moral privilege that places dominant white society outside of the web of violence and social responsibility. (Giroux 1996:56)

Giroux finds considerable fault with educators and the education system, which ignores the relevance of popular culture as a serious object of knowledge. "Wedded to the modernist infatuation with reason, mainstream educators have had little to say about the affective investments that mobilize student identities or how the mobilization of desire and the body is implicated in the pedagogical regulations of schooling" (Giroux 1996:14). Thus, according to Giroux, significant steps in the study of youth violence must include recognizing the everyday concerns outside of schools that shape the lives of violent youth. For example, acknowledge the reality that advertising is aimed primarily at youths, a group least able to afford the desired products. As Barkley (1998) claims,

> The marketplace has constructed our children as disembodied consumers—the ultimate atomized, disconnected spectator-buyers—with no places as persons in community with the right to be nurtured and the responsibility to behave appropriately. Given this, it is not difficult to grasp why there has been an increase in behaviours such as drug use, self-harm, inappropriate sexual behaviour, and violence. (Barkley 1998:315)

Many of the antecedent variables that contribute to violence are wide-ranging and interactive. These factors stem from biology; socialization; observational learning; cognitive reasoning; and the presence, absence or distortion of moral judgement. As Giroux points out, it is important to understand the social conditions that precipitate violent behaviour if we are to develop preventative strategies. Moreover, to fine tune our comprehension of causal factors, it is imperative that we incorporate into our understanding the perceptions and experiences of the main players in youth crime: the offenders themselves.

Strategies for Prevention

The final consideration in this discussion of youth violence is to address the "causes" and prevention of such behaviour. Because it is believed that only a small subset of the offending youth population is responsible for the majority of serious violent crime, authorities advocate focusing resources and preventative initiatives on the serious, violent and chronic youth offenders (Howell et al. 1995:12–13). However, the literature offers little in terms of concrete plans of action and most of the solutions reflect the narrow-minded philosophy of the various agencies, thus demonstrating the tenuous link between theory and practice. Traditional forms of prevention rely on the attribution of individual and group pathologies rather than a recognition of social and cultural pathologies. For example, more effective policing is deemed part of the solution to youth violence (Bala et al. 1994:4–6). *A Police Reference Manual on Youth and Violence* (Bala et al. 1994) recommends a five-point plan for Canada, beginning with a "balanced community response" to youth violence. This entails obtaining reliable information and an accurate understanding of the situation, but there is, unfortunately, no indication of how to accomplish this. The manual explains that professionals involved in responding to youth crime—police, Crown prosecutors, judges, probation officers and defence counsels—must consider a range of factors including the offence, as well as the youth's character, previous record and family situation. There must be care in addressing the victim's needs and in ensuring that due process is understood and followed. Lastly, a "problem-solving approach" should be utilized to "group individuals and related incidents and identify them as problems" (Bala et al. 1994:6). Once the problems are analyzed, an appropriate response to the underlying circumstances can be given. This vague description of what needs to be done does not indicate how more policing and surveillance will address the social conditions of poverty and other variables that contribute to violence. It is symptomatic of much of the literature on youth violence that there is rarely a concrete plan of action to prevent violence or any comprehension of the world as it is experienced by the youths in question.

Psychology has also experimented with types of prevention, which entail various forms of individual therapy. Play therapy, for example, allows "the inarticulate damaged child to use the child's best language, the language of play, as a form of metaphoric expression, communication and coping" (Herman et al 1995:65). This symbolic playing is verbally acknowledged by the therapist, empathized, clarified and interpreted. "This provides an empathic, supportive, and interpersonal medium for children to work through their psychopathology by correcting their distorted inner perceptions and expectation of self, others, and the world" (Herman et al. 1995:65).

There have been several evaluations of the programs designed to treat, as opposed to prevent, violent youth behaviour. Lipsey (1992) has conducted the most comprehensive review to date. His analysis indicates that youth in treatment groups have recidivism rates about 10 percent lower than those of untreated youth (cited in Howell et al. 1995:27). He claims that the most effective treatment programs in his study focused on changing overt behaviour by designing interventions to improve interpersonal relations, self-control, school achievement and job skills. More psychologically oriented treatment programs, such as individual, family and group counselling, and related practices, such as advocacy and social casework, showed only moderate positive effects. Vocational counselling and deterrence programs were least effective. In fact, "[d]eterrence programs, such as shock incarceration and those based on encounters with hard-core prisoners, actually had negative effects" (Howell et al. 1995:28). Treatment programs within the institutions appeared to be as effective as community-based programs and probation. Lipsey (1992) concludes that rehabilitative programs work, and rather than wasting efforts debating the issue, researchers, practitioners and policy-makers should move forward in developing, identifying and making available effective programs. Once again, however, there is no indication of what constitutes effective programming.

Increasing violence in schools have prompted suggestions for in-classroom prevention techniques that reinforce the notion of violence as an individual pathology. For example, Pynoos and Nader (1990) found that "classroom-conducted therapy in the wake of violent behaviour in the school can be an effective response to the post-traumatic stress experienced by children directly exposed to school violence" (cited in O'Donoghue 1995:103). Early detection is tantamount to prevention. An effective tool for administration has been a checklist of attitudinal characteristics administered to school personnel and students. A Canadian investigation (Cusson 1990) reports that "in certain contexts an experience-based code of expectations derived from an analysis of events occurring in the environment outside the school can serve as an effective guide in lowering rates of school violence" (cited in O'Donoghue 1995:105).

Perhaps more as a response to, rather than a prevention of, youth violence is the current trend to treat serious, violent youth with "get tough" policies (Lilly et al. 1995:220), such as attendance at "boot camps," for example. This again reflects the objectification of youth offenders and their lived experiences. In addition, the justice system treats some violent youth as adults by transferring their cases to adult court. The judge bases the decision to transfer on factors outlined in the Young Offenders Act: the seriousness of the alleged offence; the young person's maturity, character and offence history; pre-disposition reports; and availability of treatment. However, in practice, very few violent offence cases are transferred to adult court. According to Statistics Canada, in 1990–91, youth court judges (excluding those in Ontario) transferred 23 of 9013 violent cases, including 7 aggravated assaults, 5 sexual assaults, 5 robberies, 3 murders, 2 minor assaults and 1 weapons case. Compare this to the 48 transfers made in 1986–88 (Frank 1992:7). Similarly, in the United States the majority of juveniles in adult prisons are incarcerated for property or drug crimes; "transfer is not being applied primarily to cases of serious violent offending, as most people have assumed" (Howell et al. 1995:20).

Despite the current infrequency of transfers to adult court, the social and political response to young offenders includes a demand for tougher sanctions. For example, on March 11, 1999, Justice Minister Anne McLellan introduced the new Youth Criminal Justice Act (Bill C-3). The proposed legislation will replace the Young Offenders Act and will give more adult sentences to the most serious, violent offenders (Department of Justice, Canada 1999:5). Experts on the subject of juvenile justice see the future as a time of compromise. "On the one hand, they expect better rehabilitative treatment for those involved in less serious, less violent crime; on the other, harsher treatment for more violent offenders" (Gelber 1990 cited in Merlo 1995:115). Unfortunately this approach ignores numerous studies which indicate that severity of punishment does not deter criminal behaviour. Moreover, it fails to acknowledge the position, social circumstances and perspective of the offender, as well as the broader culture of violence in which the youth lives. These are important considerations even when offending behaviour is not occurring. As Lefer (1984) recommends, preventative strategies should address the needs of young people, their feelings of alienation, invisibility and lack of impact even when they are not committing acts of violence. This may be accomplished through conflict resolution community programs (Chisholm 1995:56).

Giroux's cultural studies approach addresses these concerns by furthering the idea of the school as a site of prevention. He claims that his book "attempts to reclaim the importance of critical pedagogy as an eminently political discourse and practice" (Giroux 1996:11). It does so, he says, by engaging how youths are being constructed in a culture that is oppressive and resistant and in which violence is seen as a legitimate practice in defining one's identity; "shaped within unequal relations of power and diasporic in its constant struggle for narrative space, culture becomes the site where youth make sense of themselves and others" (Giroux 1996:15).

Giroux claims that cultural studies should be made a primary area of study through which the construction of youth as a social category is analyzed. Cultural studies challenge educators' ideas of the importance of objectivity and their claims of ideological and political neutrality concerning the production and circulation of texts.

> Cultural studies is profoundly important for educators in that it focuses on media, not merely in terms of how it distorts and misrepresents reality, but also on how media play a part in the formation, in the constitution, of the things they reflect. (Giroux 1996:51)

Thus, alternative understandings of how violence is produced, framed aesthetically and circulated would be developed. This would allow children and youth to distinguish between violence of the spectacle and the compassion that allows them to identify with the suffering of others, to display empathy and to examine their own ethical commitments (Giroux 1996:59).

> How youth are seen through popular representations becomes indicative of how they are viewed by mainstream society and points to pedagogical practices that offer youth themselves images through which to construct their own identities and mediate their perceptions of other youth formations. (Giroux 1996:23)

It is obvious that much of the confusion in prevention strategies stems from our failure to understand the perspective of violent youths. A continual emphasis on more patrolling or individual treatment may not coincide with what the youths deem helpful. For this reason, an approach that includes the insights of youths themselves has the potential to broaden the range and diversity of options that might be employed in youth crime prevention. An understanding of what precipitates violence, and how to prevent it, is best gained through the testimony of those who have first-hand experience as perpetrators of youth crime.

Conclusion

A review of existing literature on youth violence underscores the fact that there is a void in the information. And, although part of that void is filled by the cultural studies and critical and social constructionist literature, these disciplines do not go far enough in recognizing the perspective of youth themselves. The debate between Carrington (1995) and Corrado and Markwart (1994) over the rate of youth violence reflects little more than number manipulation. Both fail to recognize that statistics are socially constructed. As Acland (1995) correctly points out, statistics are a better reflection of the politics of those who are defining them than they are an indication of the number of violent incidents. Although this is a valuable critique of the social relations underpinning the "panic" in society, it does not recognize the perspective of those whom the numbers describe.

As with statistics, the definition of youth violence also reflects the person or institution doing the defining and therefore is subjective rather than objective. Because many of the definitions and "classifications" of violent youths are developed in psychology, there is often a focus on individual pathology. Giroux indicates that there are other structural constraints associated with a "fugitive culture." In addition, it is recognized that media play a huge role in defining the violent offender. Schissel (1997) takes this idea one step further in addressing the political and economic motivation behind such portraits. But nowhere do we find the voice of the defined. Similarly, a debate over contributing factors to youth violence entails a focus on the individual. Although Giroux (1996) again outlines structural and cultural concerns that affect a youth's life, the concerns reflect Giroux's perspective. Obviously, the youths who experience the violence are not respected as "knowers" of their situation. Preventative mechanisms are also focused on the individual. Giroux claims that we need to teach kids how portraits describing them are constructed; but this does not uncover the extent to which the kids reject or appropriate such perceptions. A discussion on prevention seems pointless unless we fully understand what would be helpful to those whose behaviour we are trying to prevent or modify.

The literature clearly illustrates the need for a new approach to understanding youth violence, and this need stems from a dearth of knowledge about the perspective of those we are trying to explain. As will be outlined in Chapter Two, our failure to acknowledge the voice of youth is an extension of the fact that "children are rarely seen as competent articulators of their own experiences" (Jenks 1982 cited in James and Jenks 1996:329). In addition, as indicated in the Canadian *Police Reference Manual on Youth and Violence* (cited in Bala et al. 1994:21), the description of police procedures and the special rights afforded to youth "reflect the premise that adolescents are vulnerable and less knowledgeable than adults." As Qvortrup (1990) argues, although the right to be heard is part of the struggle for democracy, many adults say that children currently have more power than they deserve or than is good for them. In contrast, the need to value youths' opinions is the premise of this study. The theoretical and methodological principles used to accomplish this task are the focus of the next chapter.

Notes

1. The classification of a physical or sexual assault is characterized by three levels of severity. Level 1 includes common assault, which, in general, is defined by the Criminal Code as the "intentional application of force to another person, or the attempt or threat thereof" (s. 265). Level 2 involves a weapon or "bodily harm" and is defined as "any hurt or injury to the complainant that interferes with the health or comfort of the complainant, and that is more than merely transient or trifling in nature" (s. 267(2)). Level 3 involves "aggravated" assault, which is defined as that which "wounds, maims, disfigures or endangers the life of the complainant" (ss. 268, 273) (cited in Carrington 1995:66–67).

Chapter Two

The Voice of Youth
Theoretical and Methodological Imperatives

The literature on youth violence indicates a need not only for further study but, more importantly, for an entirely different approach to the subject. Much of this need arises from the inability to fully comprehend a topic based solely on the perspective of establishment authority. Current perceptions of what constitutes a "child," and "youth" in general, are based on traditional adult ideas that disregard the voice of young people. In her book, *The Everyday World as Problematic: A Feminist Sociology* (1987), Dorothy Smith explains that the marginalization and indeed silencing of particular groups of people are maintained through the "ruling apparatus" or the relations that regulate society. Although Smith uses this idea primarily in reference to a specific adult population, it is applicable to all disempowered groups, including young people. Current reaction to youth violence is one of intolerance and inability to comprehend. The societal panic that has developed over youth violence functions, according to Acland (1995), to maintain social order. Hence, there is little attempt to understand the problem, much less the perspective of youths themselves. Criminology has not listened sufficiently to the voice of violent youth, nor has it paid much attention to the way that voice is written into texts.

By doing a comparative analysis of the perspectives of establishment authority and youth offenders on the issue of violence, my approach safeguards the voice of respondents, which Smith (1987) and like-minded theorists regard as paramount in countering the hegemony of professional discourse. My intention is to outline the theoretical and methodological approach on which the data collection for this study is based.

Historical Account

Smith's (1987) "standpoint feminist" approach recognizes that women's voices and descriptions of their everyday experiences have not been included in the making of sociological categories. Although Smith applies standpoint feminism in examining the marginalization and silencing of women in particular, it can also be extended to the study of children/youth due to their similar subordinate positions. As Hardman

(1973:85) indicates in her work on the anthropological comparison between children and women, both may be referred to as "muted groups" (cited in James and Prout 1990:7).

Exploring historical categorizations of young people is important to understanding current perceptions as well as to revealing the lack of voice for children/youth in those perceptions. Over the course of time, several ideas have emerged on what constitutes a "child," none of which has taken into account the perceptions of children themselves. For example, although the Puritans emphasized children's original sin, Rousseau thought of them as free from corruption because of their inherent innocence (James 1993:72). During the Enlightenment, children were seen to be the messengers of Reason, corrupted only through increased experience in society. Locke explained that children's innocence was not innate but a consequence of their lack of social experience. The fact is that, "[a]lthough formulated in the eighteenth-century, these perceptions of the child's moral nature and development have retained a powerful and persuasive hold upon the public imagination, reappearing in different guises and with different consequences for children themselves" (James and Jenks 1996:319).

To illustrate the consequences of adult perceptions, James and Jenks (1996) cite the abuse that arose from Freud's work on childhood sexuality and from the nineteenth-century social reformers who attempted to rescue the Romantic notion of childhood by saving children from exploitive factory labour. These examples show how the notion of "innocence" has been associated with the child, "confirming its cultural identity as a passive and unknowing dependent [sic], and as therefore a member of a social group disempowered, but for good, altruistic reason" (James and Jenks 1996:320). Notions of childhood innocence and lack of responsibility are ideals that allow adults to justify children's marginal position and deny their personhood (Carrithers, Collins and Lukes 1985; Hockey and James 1993 cited in James 1993:75). Consequently, they must rely on adults to represent them. Children have little opportunity to express their views, or indeed be heard, and are vulnerable to the representations that others impose on them.

> Children's words may continue to be viewed with suspicion, or indifference, by an adult experience as in cases of child sexual abuse where age, rather than experience, may still often be deemed the more important indicator of a child's ability to tell, or even know, the truth. (James and Jenks 1996:329)

Even when young people are asked their opinion, their perspectives are seldom deemed insightful but rather are nullified by adult listeners.

Similar to the historical situation of women, children, as Allison James explains, are not conceived as persons; they have no central or active role and their words carry no effective power in the social world (1993:71).

Similarly, the classification of "youth" also conjures ideals about a group that has no voice in how they are perceived. In researching the development of youth, Aries (1962) recognized the growth of a variety of institutions, including boarding schools and military academies, as places where the young learned what it meant to enter the adult world. Modern youth was and is therefore associated with adult ideas of discipline and enforcement of order. Acland explains:

> The experience of social change engendered by modernity is inseparable from the appearance and treatment of youth. As this separate social category began to be taken as "natural," youth connoted change and became a site of both the fears and promises offered by that change. (1995:26)

Thus, the term "youth" is based on adult concepts reflecting more the aspirations and fears of the adult world than the experiences of youths themselves. The lack of adult understanding surrounding young people is reflected in the struggle to name and describe them, which indicates the current importance of this anomalous social group. Acland (1995) points to the rapid adoption of the term "Generation X" into popular vernacular after the 1991 publication of Douglas Coupland's novel *Generation X: Tales for an Accelerated Culture* (Acland 1995:145). Although "Generation X" is now used to describe those born in the 1970s, the marking of X suggests that what was indescribable has been given a semiotic visibility. Acland argues that it is but one indication of the centrality of youth in crisis in American popular culture and politics. Our younger generation is sometimes referred to as "Generation Y" or "Net Gen" (*Vancouver Sun* 1997c:E19), but the important point is that "generation" itself has no fundamental meaning except as a construction used to distinguish between at least two ambiguously defined age groups. "Generations are discursive constructs, marshalling certain meanings and desires into a single imagined location, rather than statistical truths pure and simple" (Acland 1995:25).

More recent attempts to study young people have done little to correct the lack of voice. James (1993) discusses the different sociological / anthropological approaches to studying children, which in varying degrees ignore the child's own perspective. Traditional socialization theory, for example, credits different biological aspects of childhood with determining roles in behaviour. For example, according to MacKay (1973), when socialization works well, the child becomes social; when it fails, the child becomes deviant (cited in James 1993:76). Because this socialization theory assumes that childhood is a normative process—one that posits as natural society's aspirations—it rarely documents children's own thoughts. "In this way therefore, the theoretical marginalization of the child inherent in accounts of socialization unquestioningly mirrored children's own everyday social experiences of limited participation in and access to adult society" (James 1993:76).

Although culture and personality theorists consider children to be valuable informants, the main concern of their approach has been the process and outcome of cultural reproduction as opposed to the children's own understandings of cultural processes (see for example Mead 1928; Benedict 1955). They too saw the child's social significance in terms of the future, as opposed to his or her lived reality. Thus, "[a]lthough the childhood which children experience is regarded as central to any discussion of the reproduction of cultural knowledge, how children receive and make use of that knowledge remains relatively uncharted" (James 1993:82). We learn from both historical and present descriptions of young people that not only do they lack a voice in the production of ideas about them, but also that adult theories directly infringe upon how they experience their own childhood (James 1993:72).

Hence, past theories and perspectives on young people have both reflected and perpetuated their marginal position in society. Innocence, dependency and discipline are attributes that, to the present, have defined how children are expected to behave. Youths who fall outside these socially defined boundaries are perceived as bad or delinquent, which stems from an ignorance of the youths' viewpoint. Because the personal perspective of young people is rarely valued, adults continue to impose their understanding upon how youths experience everyday life.

The Ruling Apparatus

Smith's (1987) notion of "ruling apparatus" (or relations of ruling) is central to understanding how adult perceptions of young people are formed and maintained. The term "ruling apparatus" "brings into view the intersection of the institutions organizing and regulating society…; a concept that grasps power, organization, direction, and regulation as more pervasively structured than can be expressed in traditional concepts provided by the discourses of power" (Smith 1987:3). The ruling apparatus comprises the total complex of powerful institutions—management, government, the intelligentsia and other establishment agencies—as well as the social rationalization for its existence. Reflective of its power, it has the capacity to organize and integrate places, persons and events into a societal whole by using systems, rules, laws and conceptual dictums or practices (Smith 1987:108).

The overall character of the ruling apparatus depends upon the social relations that organize and enforce the silence of those who do not participate in the process of naming. The form of childhood is shaped by systems of meanings and processes from which writers and social theorists of childhood are not immune. As Smith (1987:17) indicates, how we think about ourselves, each other and society is shaped and distributed by the specialized work of people in universities, media, advertising and other agencies forming what Althusser calls the "ideological apparatuses" of the society. "The writer, enmeshed in language ... is inevitably enmeshed in ideology and, as professional peddlers of words, such persons are involved in its re-creation" (James 1993:74). This means that, because youths have been excluded from the production of ideology, knowledge and culture, their experience and ways of knowing are not represented in the organization of ruling. "The silence of those outside the apparatus is a silence in part materially organized by the pre-emption, indeed virtual monopoly, of communications media and the educational process as part of the ruling apparatus" (Smith 1987:57). For example, psychology has continued to emphasize "rationality" over personal experience, and psychiatry provides a set of techniques for examining one's life and experience in relation to an ideology that legitimates conformities of feelings.

Smith's theory draws on Marx's and Engels' account of ideology,

> [which] provides a method enabling us to see how ideas and social forms of consciousness may originate outside experience, coming from an external source and becoming a forced set of categories into which we must stuff the awkward and resistant actualities of our worlds. (1987:55)

Herein the concept of ideology directs us to search for the practical organization of the production of images and symbols and to examine the origins of the social forms of consciousness. Ideas of the ruling class penetrate and dominate the social consciousness.

According to Smith, gender, although assumed neutral, is a social construct that supports the ruling apparatus; so too is the notion of childhood/youth (Boyden 1990). As Ambert (1986) suggests, "children's relative absence is rooted in the same factors which excluded attention to women (and gender): that is, a male-dominated sociology that does not give worth to child care and still less to the activities of children themselves" (cited in James and Prout 1990:23). The way we understand ourselves and society is part of the relations of ruling, and it stems therefore from positions of power occupied mainly by adult males, more specifically, white, heterosexual, affluent males. Men are invested with the authority to make what they say count, not as individuals with expertise but as men, who represent the power of the institutionalized structures that govern (Smith 1987:30). Women, in contrast, have taken for granted that their thinking is authorized by external authoritative sources and, consequently, their opinions conform to the approved standards set by men. Thus, women's opinions, like those of young people, are separated from their daily experience (Smith 1987:35).

There is an ever-increasing focus on the disjuncture between children's own experiences and the institutional form that childhood takes (James and Prout 1990 cited in James and Jenks 1996:317). Various statutes habitually shape the "pacing and placing" of children's daily routine. For example, school restricts their access to social space; and, due to dominant pediatric and psychological theories of child development (Jenks 1982), children are obliged by the adult world to be happy and well adjusted. There is a gap between children's everyday life and the means they have to express themselves.

Smith refers to these two modes of knowing, experiencing and acting, as a "bifurcation of consciousness" or movement between a consciousness organized within the relations of ruling and a consciousness connected to daily life (1987:7). The ordinary social processes of socialization, education, work and communication have a repressive effect. For instance, in an ideologically structured society, education teaches children the skills they need to participate, as well as the imperative to accept and support forms of relations dictated from outside of their own experience. Smith argues that women have learned to treat themselves as objects, to deny or obliterate their subjectivity and experience. Smith's views equally can be applied to children; young people also have "learned to live inside a discourse that is not [theirs] and that expresses and describes a landscape in which [they] are alienated and that preserves that alienation as integral to its practice" (Smith 1987:36). Due to the social construction of childhood which provides both form and content to the way young people relate and are related to in everyday life, "children are locked, for their intelligibility within the contingency of social convention. The negotiable character of these conventions is a question of power, which children exercise only in a partial form. They can demand attention but not redefinition" (James and Jenks 1996:319).

Hence, childhood remains a subjugated experience in which children have rights to safety but not to autonomy (Ennew 1986:21 cited in James and Jenks 1996:318). Acland argues that the rhetoric over a concern for youths' best interests stems from an "ideology of protection" (1995:25). Because youth is a time when culture is learned, it is also a time of surveillance. The ideology of protection inevitably means control and manipulation of the child by adult authorities for the purpose of maintaining status-quo social relations (Acland 1995:25).

Although the ruling apparatus depends upon silencing those people who do not participate in creating ideology, we must consider that people might not always interpret their own situation as oppressive. Relations of ruling involve a covert process that is often not obvious, particularly to those for whom it is disadvantageous. According to Smith's notion that consciousness about youth exists outside of the youths' experience, they may comprehend the everyday world much differently from what is presumed. Rather than excluding their voice from the production of knowledge, incorporating the perspective of young people would add new insight. This is especially important in the attempt to understand the problem of, and response to, youth violence.

Current Reaction to Violent Youth Crime

Historically, hegemonic views of young people arising from, and perpetuated by, the ruling apparatus have contributed to adult intolerance of certain groups without consideration of their voice. In particular, these views have led to societal panic over the supposed frequency and nature of youth violence. Rather than recognizing the value of incorporating violent youths' perspective into solutions, adults often respond with harsher treatment and other forms of regulation and control. It appears that violent youths fall between the protectionist realm of "childness" and the rights discourse of "adultness" and therefore disentitled to the securities afforded to either.

A good example of the notion of childhood as "innocence enshrined"— and how young people who deviate are no longer considered children— is evident in the reaction to the infamous Bulger murder in 1993. This case took place in Britain and involved two ten-year-old boys who lured four-year-old James Bulger away from his mother in a shopping mall, beat the child to death and placed his body across the railway line so it would be run over by a train. James and Jenks examine "public reaction [to the murder] in terms of mass media content, against a general ignorance of the actual child's point of view" (1996:315). They explain that the murder was not only disturbing, but unthinkable because of the age of the offenders.

Children who commit violent crimes disrupt our concept of "the child" and force an examination of the socially constructed nature of childhood. Understanding children as intrinsically dependent and pure is what makes any connection between children and violent crime problematic, "for the imagery of childhood and that of violent criminality are iconologically irreconcilable" (James and Jenks 1996:320). The response is often "conceptual eviction;" we exclude those children who commit violent acts from the category of "childhood" altogether (James and Jenks 1996:322). We describe them as "evil freaks" or "little devils" with "adult" brains and demand that they be charged and sentenced as adults. Note the reaction to the murder of British Columbia's fifteen-year-old Reena Virk, who was severely beaten by a group of girls, assaulted by a male and female youth; and subsequently left for dead in the George waterway in Sannich near Victoria. Professional and public demand is that the two teenaged murderers be tried in adult court. Lacking the innocence of a child and the maturity of an adult, the violent teen defies traditional categorization. (S)he is "Other" on two counts: (s)he is the "adult-child" who is inherently evil.

This identification of Otherness is an essential element in the establishment of social order. "[T]hrough their remarked differences [violent youth] work to firm up the boundaries which give form and substance to the conceptual categories from which they are excluded" (James and Jenks 1996:323). The creation of the Other is integral to both the notion of "youth in crisis" (Acland 1995) and the preservation of a particular social order. Social order stems from how a culture "thinks" itself.

> The result is a mobile, conflictual fusion of power, fear and desire in the construction of subjectivity: a psychological dependence upon precisely those Others which are being rigorously opposed and excluded at the societal level. It is for this reason that what is socially peripheral is so frequently symbolically central. (Stallybrass and White 1986:5 cited in Acland 1995:19)

Acland (1995) illustrates that particular "cultural sites," such as those occupied by violent youth, are invested with significant connotative force. Even though such sites are outside the bounds of society and are seen as Other, they are inseparable from and, in fact, construct the social order. Distinctions between the social order and Otherness are dependent on feelings of disgust and desire: "while youth is 'other' in the adult world, it is also an object of intense interest, desire, even longing, for the culture as a whole" (Acland 1995:19). Acland (1995) explains that these sentiments provide the impetus for the development of a concept of "youth in crisis" through a focus on "the spectacular." There is a systematic progression from the initial violent acts of youth to their emergence as the focus of news coverage, talk shows and youth movies. Acland (1995) claims that it is in this increasing media attention, or "movements," that the historical specificity of "youth in crisis" arises. He employs the term "the politics of spectacle" to describe how violent crime committed by youths is represented and circulated in newspaper and media so that, "even as the initial crime is left behind, a general crisis of youth is being established" (Acland 1995:14). Thus, crimes do not stand alone but occur in particular contexts situated in discursive environments (Acland 1995:21).

Acland discusses how discourses on youth violence have implications for the forms and specifics of "the popular" at a given moment and how they are deployed, in essence, to serve a cultural purpose (1995:10). Why certain crimes become symbolically important at a particular moment is a function of the broader social apparatus. The import of crime is also predicated on the distribution of social power. Acland (1995) questions how the social construction of youth crime figures into the establishment, form and reproduction of societal order. He cites Paul Willis (1977:179), who characterized the irreducible relation between the material and the conceptual as a primary force behind the transformation of order:

> [c]ultural forms cannot be reduced or regarded as the mere epiphenomenal expression of basic structural factors. They are not accidental or open-ended determined variables in the couplet structure / culture. They are part of the necessary circle in which neither term is thinkable alone. It is in the passage through the cultural level that aspects of the real structural relationships of society are transformed into conceptual relationships and back again. The culture is part of the necessary dialectic of reproduction. (cited in Acland 1995:12)

Acland uses Willis' idea of the dialectic of reproduction to understand the distribution of social power according to discourses of gender, race, class and age. The understanding of these variables is transformed through social relations in the attempt to maintain order. This is illustrated, for example, in the panic caused by the young age of those committing murder. It seems that the voice of youth is excluded from the discourse on youth violence because it does not serve the purpose of law and order that "youth in crisis" fosters. In fact, young people's perspectives may dismantle the constructs that feed societal panic. As Acland (1995:13) asserts, "youth in crisis" is fabricated to serve the larger cultural and structural purpose of maintaining social order.

Similarly, Schissel draws on Stanley Cohen's (1980) concept of "moral panic," contending that "public panics are predictable in that they have little to do with a criminogenic reality and much to do with the economic and political context in which they arise" (Schissel 1997:10). He argues that the current political pastime of "blaming children" is fuelled by two phenomena. The first is the increase in visibility of young people in public places as a consequence of youth unemployment. The presence of kids in shopping malls, for example, elicits panic that youths are loitering with the aim of committing crime. The second is that most Canadians derive their opinions about the extent of youth crime from the news, which, filtered through American media, "is sensational, selective to time and place, and focuses primarily on the dangerous" (Schissel 1997:11). The result is a gap between the reality that there has been little real increase in serious youth crime and the perception that it is out of control.

> [T]he panic that vilifies children is a coordinated and calculated attempt to nourish the ideology that supports a society stratified on the bases of race, class and gender, and ... the war on kids is part of the state-capital mechanism that continually reproduces an oppressive social and economic order. (Schissel 1997:10)

Thus, Canada is on the verge of a moral panic that may lead to the indictment of all adolescents, with specific consequences for those who are disadvantaged.

Another societal response to violent youth crime is to trace its source to particular microcosmic factors. There is a continual search in the literature for somebody or something to blame for violent youth: video games, violent movies, dysfunctional families, declining standards of morality and discipline. In many cases, these scapegoats tend to be simplistic, one-dimensional explanations of convenience, rooted in popular myth. Moreover, because the search for solutions to youth violence excludes the perspective of youths themselves, such inquiries are more an attempt to temporarily alleviate societal panic than to develop strategies aimed at resolving the problem. Individual explanations also illuminate society's need to safeguard the traditional notion of what constitutes a child. James and Jenks indicate that throughout modernity the child was protected because (s)he symbolized the future; but given our currently diminished belief in progress and future, they postulate that the child now symbolizes the stability of the past and is defended only through nostalgia (1996:324).

A need to reaffirm the "normal" child has resulted in increased supervision of children's activities and in more visible forms of containment. The typical governmental response to the growing moral panic has been to establish more controls on behaviour. In Vancouver, special police and probation units have been formed to deal with the issue of violent, gang-affiliated youth. Similarly, the policy of transferring youths to adult court for extreme cases of violence has been implemented nationwide.

Recently, an article entitled "Violent youth, crime victims top justice minister's agenda" appeared in the *Vancouver Sun* (1997b). In it Justice Minister Anne McLellan states that "[c]oncern about violent crime is growing and faith in the justice system's ability to deal with this problem is decreasing" (1997b:A1). McLellan promises to take a "hard look" at the youth system: "Violent youth crime demands a strong response.... Canadians must have confidence that there will be a firm response to serious offences committed by young offenders" (*Vancouver Sun* 1997b:A15). In keeping with Foucault's (1979) notion of the watchtower, "[s]uch a response addresses not the moral grounds of the problem but rather defers this question through the modern recourse to further surveillance in the place of understanding" (James and Jenks 1996:321).

It appears that the response to violent children is twofold; on the one hand are calls for greater punishment and revenge, and on the other are demands for care and understanding. A newspaper article entitled "Charging children young as 10 recommended in MPs' study" (*Vancouver Sun* 1997a) details proposals to implement stricter legislation dealing with young people who commit crime.

> Despite recommending some changes to toughen the act, a draft of the committee report strongly urges the retention of a separate youth justice system to treat young offenders differently from adult criminals because "they are not yet fully formed people." (*Vancouver Sun* 1997a:A4)

There is obvious confusion in public perceptions of what young people need. "[W]e do not know what actions to take because we do not know what children are ... therefore we can neither understand nor articulate their needs" (James and Jenks 1996:327).

Overall, it appears that the reaction to youth violence is saturated with ambiguity and contradiction. On one hand, there are desperate attempts to uncover the contributing factors, and, on the other, it would be uneconomical and socially disruptive if solutions were implemented. "Youth in crisis" has contributed to societal panic but, at the same time, it is an industry sustained by sensationalist media. The details of gruesome, hideous and unbelievable crime have always interested the wider public. The Bulger murder would never have received such pervasive coverage had the details of the crime been less shocking. And, because the most violent crimes are highlighted and publicized to a disproportionate extent, even though there may be a small number of violent youth, there is a societal perception of rampant crime. Moreover, the exclusion of violence from the classification of the "child" strengthens and reaffirms traditional constructs of childhood.

Considering the responses to youth violence, it is perhaps not surprising that the voice of those involved is rarely deemed valuable. Listening to youths' perceptions would undoubtedly reveal a need to examine adult constructs of young people and to re-evaluate current methods of dealing with violent offenders.

Hearing the Voice of Youth

James and Jenks (1996) recommend investigating why children commit acts of violence by learning from children themselves about crime and violence. They recognize how important this idea was when, during the 1980s, sexual abuse was high on the agenda: "[W]e found that we did not know much about the extent of children's knowledge about sex, so too now the adult world finds itself in a state of ignorance about what ordinary children do ordinarily to one another" (James and Jenks 1996:328). In an article entitled "Decision-making critical to youth: child advocate" (*Saskatoon Star-Phoenix* 1997), the province's Children's Advocate, Deborah Parker-Loewen, argued that ensuring children's involvement in the decisions that affect them was the foremost issue facing Saskatchewan youth. Although young people usually do not contact adult institutions, Parker-Loewen was impressed that 20 percent of the calls to her in 1996 had been from children, indicating youths' increasing participation in decision-making: "It's a form of respect and a valuing of young people to include them" (*Saskatoon Star-Phoenix* 1997:A3). Further, her office promoted policies to eliminate corporal punishment from Saskatchewan schools, which, she claimed, would promote the respect and dignity of Saskatchewan youth. Some of the recommendations in Parker-Loewen's annual report released at the legislature appear as a result of complaints from young people demanding that children's voices be heard, respected and answered.

During the 1960s anthropologist Charlotte Hardman was one of the first to argue for child-centred approaches, which saw children as "people to be studied in their own right and not just as receptacles of adult teaching" (1973:87 cited in James 1993:85). The paradigm begins with children as active participants in the social world where they partake in shaping their own lives. The appeal of this approach is that it allows children to have a "direct voice and participation in the production of sociological data" and to be "active in the construction and determination of their own social lives, the lives of those around them and of the societies in which they live" (James and Prout 1990:8)

Although ethnographic studies are a welcome advance in the study of children, it is crucial to recognize that such accounts are not ideologically neutral or unproblematic. They both reflect and contribute to creating a climate of opinion about childhood, which can perpetuate the conceptual marginality of children (James 1993:88). Moreover, the constructions of childhood become increasingly distanced from the social, economic and political institutions of everyday life. For example, there are several published autobiographical accounts of childhood, but these books centre on their authors' memories of childhood rather than on childhood from the standpoint of diverse children (see, for example, Foley 1974; Gamble 1979).

> The child that the author was becomes a symbol of and for all children and all childhoods of that social class and historical period ... [D]espite their individualising of childhood through personal biography, these accounts also participate in generalizing and homogenising the category of children. (James 1993:90)

The fact that we still talk of "the child" and legislate on behalf of children through laws such as the Young Offenders Act illustrate the continuing denial by adults of children's subjectivity. In the adult world, age, gender, class, disability and ethnicity are important analytical characteristics, yet these are not identified in qualifying the category of child. In her study of how children experience illness and disability, Allison James indicates that, through interviews with the parents of these children, she gained insight into the social construction of childhood and its dependency upon relations of power, authority and social control. Yet she learned little of the children's own experiences:

> What these differing strategies clearly reveal is the subtlety of social encounters in a society defined largely by and for its adult members. In these interviews (which were later to contrast so strongly with those in which children themselves defined the form and content), I was unwittingly drawn into replicating this marginalization. Thus, the few glimpses which the interviews provide into what it feels like to be a child who is in some way regarded as significantly different must be tempered by the relationships of power and authority which frame the social context of its voicing. (James 1993:92)

The importance of listening to the voice of youths is increasingly being recognized. Not only is it deemed significant in better understanding their perspective but, perhaps more importantly, it also makes young people feel that they are valued and contributing members of society. However, as indicated in previous studies, the approach used in "listen-

44

ing to youth" is not without complication. To overcome adult-centred interpretations and covert relations of power, it is essential to employ a methodology that allows youth to speak from, and be appreciated for, their own perspective.

Research Method

The main intent of this study is to address the lack of youth's voice through a method—rather than a methodology—that protects their perspective in the discourse on violent crime. Smith's (1987) work is especially pertinent in accomplishing this aim. Her approach is not a totalizing theory but rather *"a method of inquiry … relevant to the politics and practice of progressive struggle, whether of women or other oppressed groups"* (1992:88, her emphasis). The project begins in the actualities of youths' experiences.

To further Smith's argument (1987), there is a need to explore the everyday world from the "standpoint"[1] of youth. This entails beginning from a "point of rupture," recognizing the experience of youth within social forms of consciousness and comparing it to how the world feels, senses and responds to the youth experience. "From this starting point, the next step locates that experience in the social relations organizing and determining precisely the disjuncture, that line of fault along which the consciousness of [youth] must emerge" (Smith 1987:49). The standpoint approach cannot be equated with perspective or worldview. It does not universalize a particular experience but rather is a method that,

> at the outset of inquiry, creates the space for an absent subject, and an absent experience that is to be filled with the presence and spoken experience of actual [youth] speaking of and in the actualities of their everyday worlds. (Smith 1987:107)

The standpoint of youth is situated outside textually mediated discourses of professionals and is found in the actualities of the life experience of youth. Although it is not entirely attainable, the standpoint of youth implies a study that begins, not with detached "scientific consciousness" but in a prior context, in which the researcher and subject ideally co-exist on the same basis. In taking the standpoint of youth, the researcher is brought into defined relations with youths whose experiences will be expressed in the research. At the same time, "the concepts and frameworks, our methods of inquiry, of writing texts, and so forth are integral aspects of that relation" (Smith 1987:111). The professional discourse on youth violence applies equally to that everyday moment in which I encounter the youths. It is important to appreciate that the relations with the youths are organized by the inquiry.

The disjuncture that provides the problematic of this inquiry exists between the forms of thought, symbols, images, vocabularies and institutionalized structures of society and a world experienced by youth at a level prior to the expression and knowledge of establishment authority. This study takes both the experience and perspective of youth and the perspective of establishment authority on youth and questions, first, how the difference between the two perspectives is organized and determined and, second, what the social relations are that generate it (Smith 1987:50). Thus, I will examine the actual or potential disjuncture between youths' experience and the form in which their experience is socially expressed.

The notion of "problematic" recognizes that the everyday world, as the matrix of our experience, is organized by relations that tie it to larger processes and locally organized practices. This idea is used to relate my inquiry to "the experience of members of a society as knowers located in actual lived situations in a new way" (Smith 1987:91). The conception of the everyday world as problematic presents the foundation for a study that starts with actual social relations rather than with the discourse itself. In other words, my research is concerned with violent youth and their experience expressed in their own words as opposed to the words of establishment authority. The youths' descriptions of their experience in the justice system, their homes and their schools locates the beginning of inquiry in that everyday world of youth. The concept of problematic "explicates" (allows meaning to evolve from) rather than explains (which often entails professional interpretation of) a property of the everyday world as a focus.

> [The problematic] is used here to direct attention to a possible set of questions that may not have been posed or a set of puzzles that do not yet exist in the form of puzzles but are "latent" in the actualities of the experienced world. (Smith 1987:91)

According to Smith (1987), defining the everyday world as the locus of a criminological problematic is not the same as making it an object of study or a phenomenon.

> To aim at the everyday world as an object of study is to constitute it as a self-contained universe of inquiry … [and] the effect of locating the knower in this way is to divorce the everyday world of experience from the larger social and economic relations that organize its distinctive character. (Smith 1987:90)

In other words, the intent is not to isolate everyday experience as a phenomenon in its own right. Rather, the concept of problematic is used to relate criminological inquiry directly to the experience of youth "knowers" situated in real life. It calls for a procedure emanating from the social reality of youth and progressing to a conceptualization explaining the interplay between experience and the larger context in which that experience exists. The problematic is a method of guiding and focusing inquiry, not an attempt to sever experience from the larger social relations that provide the context for experience. Hence, by eliciting the voice of youth, my study is meant to question youth offenders as "knowers" situated in their own experience and to juxtapose this knowledge base with that of establishment authority.

In addition, the concept of the problematic transfers opacity to the level of discourse by directing attention to possible sets of questions not yet posed but very real in the everyday youth experience. These areas are not recognized under normal circumstances and become evident only when they are problematized and subjected to systematic inquiry. Smith cautions that to write the youths' standpoint into texts, the researcher must supplant her "discursive privilege" in favour of the youth perspective (1987:127). However, because the relations that affect the subjects' daily experience are not readily obvious to either themselves or the researcher, the inquiry must expand beyond their point of view. The problematic, located by youths' ignorance of how their world is shaped and determined by relations and forces external to them, must not be understood to imply that they are "dopes or dupes."

> Within our everyday worlds, we [the researchers] are expert practitioners of their quiddity, of the way they [the subjects] are just the way they are. Our everyday worlds are in part our own accomplishments, and our special and expert knowledge is continually demonstrated in their ordinary familiarity and unsurprising ongoing presence. (Smith 1987:110)

But how they are woven into extended social relations is not always discernible by youth themselves; this is the task of social scientists. Due to the researcher's position and her own experiences, she should not impose her understanding onto what the youths say about their experiences. Although the youths may not realize their perspective or associate it with larger social relations, they should still be considered experts in reference to how they understand youth violence. It is up to the researcher to bring the significance of the larger social relations to light, without negating what the youths themselves have to say.

These concepts recognize that ways of thinking about youth are combined with institutionalized practices, the effect of which is the production of self-conscious subjects who perceive themselves through those ways of thinking. This study intends to examine how "official knowledge" impacts both the establishment authority and the youths and, in particular, how responses are created by regimes of truth. As Smith indicates, ways of understanding are properties of organization or discourse rather than of individual subjects (1987:3). This lends insight about the extent to which youths embody or accept the categories imposed on them, as well as the effect of resisting such classification.

For this reason, my data collection involved going through each of the youths' files, including detailed reports from various establishment authorities. According to Smith (1987), the final stage of inquiry is to expose those relations of ruling that are not explicit in what is said, or even realized, by the respondent. These extensive files contain ten main reports, which detail almost every action of a youth's daily routine. Youth Court Services staff does not overtly label the youths as violent. One psychologist, an interviewee for the study, explained that it is not a diagnostic term: "We operate with DSM-IV (1994)[2] so kids would get on their files a diagnosis but that doesn't include violent offender. That is a meaningless term, one used in the newspaper." A probation officer, also a study participant, stated that, according to Criminal Code criteria, offences, not people, are classified as "violent." There is, however, a "needs analysis" to determine risk assessment in terms of violent behaviour.

The files contain massive amounts of information, ranging from youth risk assessments and custody reports to case management reports and daily program logs, providing a valuable source for understanding how authorities interpret the youths' behaviour. According to Smith (1987), we must extend the investigation beyond the particular institution to the bureaucratic and administrative level. I therefore compared the youths' testimony to institutional files to determine differences in perception. "The aim of analysis has been to disclose a social organization implied but not spoken of in the original narratives, a social organization that is presupposed but not explicit" (Smith 1987:202).

Institutional ideologies are acquired by members as a way of analyzing experiences in the processes of the institution. "Professional training in particular teaches people how to recycle the actualities of their experience into the forms in which it is recognizable within institutional discourse" (Smith 1987:161–62). As a partial result of developments in criminology, psychology and sociology, probation officers and social workers, for example, address families in terms of interpersonal relations and roles "a language that has rendered the institutional presence of the home as a work setting for women and as an economy invisible" (Smith 1987:163).

Not all aspects of this process are transparent; institutional ideologies provide "analytic procedures for those settings that attend selectively to work processes, thus making only selective aspects of them accountable within the institutional order" (Smith 1987:162). Smith (1987) argues that, because the language of social science is the language of institutional process, we therefore cannot invest in it or depend upon its analyses to organize our inquiry.

Impediments to the Standpoint Approach

It follows that the standpoint approach stems from problems with orthodox criminological approaches. Among other things, it problematizes long-standing institutional values associated with conducting academic research. The resistance to new approaches is evident, for example, in the guidelines for ethical research at most universities. In effect, the present study of youth violence, which is based on Smith's work, runs counter to and is challenged by the disciplinary requirements and definitions entrenched in our current social sciences.

It follows that the standpoint approach was developed in response to problems with orthodox criminological approaches. For example, in traditional criminological inquiry, the need for objectivity is a requirement for successful data collection. As Smith observes, however, "we have learned a method of thinking that does away with the presence of the subjects in the phenomena, which only subjects can accomplish" (1987:74). In work informed by this conventional paradigm, the researcher interviews a "subject" who answers the question but does not tell the researcher what questions to ask and therefore is not a participant in the textually mediated discourse (Smith 1987:116). Traditional criminology has continually suppressed the presence of the subject of inquiry. "While objectivity, in the sense of the detached scientific knower, has come to be seen as an essential property of its scientific texts, actuality has continued to resist this discursive production" (Smith 1987:117). Consequently the final text is an account of the researcher's own construction of her "subjects," who stand outside of the account; it "reinterprets the daily actualities of their lives into the alienated constructs of sociological discourse, subordinating their experienced worlds to the categories of ruling" (Smith 1987:117). Classifications are imposed on people by using specific criteria to make them fit between the world and the theoretical formulation expressed in the categories (Smith 1987:131).

Again borrowing from Marx and Engels, the premises of Smith's method "can be verified in purely empirical ways" in that the social itself creates the conditions of its own observability (cited in Smith 1987:127).

There is no reliance on a technical method that produces objectivity but on an inquiry oriented by prospective questions from others.

> [Thus,] in contrast to the established methodologies construct- ing a third version out of contending versions and thus consti- tuting the objectivity of the world as a product of inquiry, we propose a method of inquiry that relies on the existence of a world in common ongoingly created and recreated in human sensuous activities ... indeed the work of inquiry itself goes forward in and is part of the same world as it explicates. (Smith 1987:127)

The standpoint approach is also incompatible with existing ethical standards, which are self-interested and antagonistic to Smith's method. For example, an administrator representing the chair of the ethics com- mittee at Simon Fraser University stated that I had to submit the question- naire for both the youths and the establishment authorities prior to interviewing. Although the interview questions, according to Smith (1987), are supposed to be derived from conversations with participants, my questions had to be determined in advance, according to institutional imperatives.

The questionnaires for both groups of respondents were designed to close gaps and clarify areas of confusion in the literature on youth violence. The questionnaire for the youths began by addressing the aftermath of the offence. This included questions about how the youths experienced particular aspects of the justice system and how various people in their lives, from family and friends to youth justice officials, reacted to their crime. In an attempt to maximize accurate recollection, the questions were sequenced to correspond to the events that generally follow a crime. The second group of questions was aimed at better understanding how the youths perceive their actions, themselves and the notion of violence. The third group of questions was related to the correctional facility and the youths' perceptions of staff and other offend- ers; programs, such as anger management; and punishment. The final section of the questionnaire was very general and open-ended to allow the youths the final word in the interview. They were asked about violence in society and, perhaps most importantly, about which areas they felt should be studied. I often asked the youths how they would deal with someone in their own situation if they were given the task and necessary resources.

The questionnaire for the establishment authorities was similarly designed to allow for a comparative analysis. The first section of ques- tions inquired into how the respondents understand both the circumstance and character of those who commit violent acts and the notion of violence in a general sense. The second section focused on the various procedures of the criminal justice system and the establishment authorities' perceptions of the responses of youth. The third section addressed programs offered to deal with violent youth, the effectiveness of treatment and ideas for alternatives. I concluded with more general questions on the rate and explanation of youth violence as well as other areas that establishment authorities indicated were important to the discussion of youth violence.

In defiance of the Simon Fraser University (SFU) ethical requirement, my methods for interviews conformed to Smith's reasoning; I allowed respondents the freedom to discuss what was of importance to them and to diverge from the questionnaires. This freedom is important because how informants tell the story of their violent experience or of their dealings with violent youth is essential to the analysis of relations of ruling (Smith 1987:187). The methodological assumption is that respondents express the relations in very ordinary ways. Smith argues that the way terms are used in their original context, including their syntax arrangements, is "controlled" or "governed" by social organization, which is an ordering procedure in how people tell others about that original setting (1987:188). Respondents were not confined to a specific set or sequence of questions. Quite often we discussed points of importance to them. Smith claims that, "given that we do not disrupt the process by the procedures we use, open-ended interviewing should … yield stretches of talk that 'express' the social organization and relations of the setting" (1987:189). While there is nothing new about open-ended interviewing, it is the use of the resulting material that is distinctive to standpoint epistemology. Traditional approaches use methods of coding and interpretation to order the interview materials in relation to the relevances of the discourse, making the standpoint that of the discourse and not that of the subject.

There were additional problems with the ethics review process. Although I understand and appreciate the need for "informed consent" from respondents, the SFU ethics committee chair asked me to guarantee consent in a way that protected the university but intimidated the respondents. For example, as part of my proposal I had to submit the exact wording of what was going to be said to each youth. I was to discourage respondents from mentioning crimes for which they had not been caught because, if subpoenaed to court, I would have to reveal everything. In addition, the chair's decisions about ethics, liability, confidentiality and epistemology were made without consulting the committee as a whole. Drs. Ted Palys and John Lowman, two SFU criminology professors, have recently cited these concerns in their call for an independent review of the entire ethics process. In a memorandum to the ethics committee (1998) Palys and Lowman state:

> [T]his case demonstrates how non-ethical criteria, particularly concerns about liability, have contaminated the ethics application process ... [and in so doing] infringed academic freedom and undermined protection of the anonymity of research participants and confidentiality of the information they provide.

The university's failure to protect both me and my participants through guarantees of strict confidentiality limited what the youths could disclose and further compromised the standpoint approach that I was endeavouring to emulate.

Traditional disciplinary approaches are antagonistic to a standpoint method because sociological discourse, and I would suggest criminological discourse too, "has maintained its hegemony over experience ... by insisting that we must begin with conceptual apparatus or a theory drawn from the discipline" (Smith 1987:89). A central component of criminological methodology is the assumption that we cannot encounter the world without a concept, "that knowing it relies on the ordering procedures already established in the theoretical armamentarium of the discourse" (Smith 1987:122). Criminology is part of the ideological structure in that the themes and relevances have been traditionally organized and articulated from the perspective of men or other authority figures. As Maureen Cain (1990) argues in outlining her strategy for a transgressive criminology, there are no "tools" in criminological theory to explore the total lives of women or, in this case, youths. Traditional criminology starts with the sites and practices "given" it by the criminal law and its administration (Garland 1985 cited in Cain 1990:10). Cain argues that "the elements of a transgressive criminology are necessary to allow for a new language that will capture [youths'] own incapable-of-being-thought-about experiences brought to consciousness in a supportive process of giving these experiences voice and (re)cognition" (Cain 1990:8).

Smith (1987) argues that the belief that one cannot examine the everyday world without a conceptual framework is an indication of how the social sciences are part of the ruling apparatus. Although the theories, concepts and methods of the discipline are purportedly capable of accounting for and analyzing the world as experienced by all, they have been developed through a hierarchized knowledge of the world that takes for granted the boundaries of experience (Smith 1987:85). "Since the procedures, methods, and aims of present sociology [and criminology] give primacy to the concepts, relevances, and topics of the discourse, we cannot begin from that frame" (Smith 1987:89).

Indicative of preconceived notions, several of the establishment authorities indicated that they understood the attitude of the youths and therefore had ideas on how I should approach them in the interviews. However, the suggestions did not ring true when I actually spoke with the youths. For example, the psychiatrist recommended that I "don't just start with 'So what did you do?'" Instead I should start with "'How's it going? Is anyone bothering you or intimidating you?' From there you will pick up what they are interested in talking about; then from there you get into a discussion about the system." He also said, "Kids are very smart and these guys have gone through so many interviews. They can recognize if you're nervous ... and they'll play on it." Another authority suggested: "Talk in their language ... ask them simple questions." Despite the advice, I still began each interview by asking the youths about the crime they had committed. Most already knew what I wanted to discuss, and I did not sense any reluctance or suspicion.

There was additional advice on how to interpret the youths' responses. Several authorities, for example, commented on the youths' credibility. One psychiatric social worker stated, "Don't expect them to be honest. They'll try to make themselves sound like a hero; they'll either justify that what they did was right or they'll completely deny it.... Independent reports such as files are good." Another psychiatric social worker said, "Make sure you are honest and straightforward; they will distrust you. Tell them that you've read their file." Even though I did not tell the youths that I had access to their files, I got the impression that they were telling me "their" truth.

The imperatives of generalizability, fundamental to traditional criminological procedure, are also incongruent with the standpoint approach. According to the orthodoxy, a purported problem with ethnographies has been that, however fascinating accounts of people's lives might be, they cannot stand as general or typical statements about society. Smith (1987) argues that beginning with an understanding of the everyday world as problematic helps to explode this conventional wisdom. She states that the linkage of the local and particular to generalized social relations is not a conceptual or methodological issue, but a property of social organization.

> The particular "case" is not particular in the aspects that are of concern to the inquirer.... The problematic of the everyday world arises precisely at the juncture of particular experience, with generalizing and abstracted forms of social relations organizing a division of labour in society at large. (Smith 1987:157)

Multiple perspectives and versions create a problem only when the project is attempting to produce a criminological version bypassing the perspective of respondents or to ground criminology in "meaning" and "common understandings" (Smith 1987:141).

What this means in terms of the present study of youth violence is that a random or other "scientific" sample is not required; there is no attempt to generalize from a small number to the characteristics of a larger population (Smith 1987:187). However, because sampling issues continue to be an important aspect of traditional research, maintaining the standpoint of youth was not easy. As with Smith's experience, it was easy to slip back into an "outsider's" standpoint (1987:185), particularly when I was setting up the interviews and was asked by those helping me what my sampling procedure was and how many youths I needed to interview. Thinking in this way creates problems of sampling and of representation of the larger population. There were definitely recurrent topics and situations, but there was no intention in the study to employ arbitrary methodology to discover the distribution of my participants as a sample. Rather, I wanted to explore how the institutional practices of establishment authority penetrate and organize the experience of individual youth. "So rather than inserting into our analysis of the interviews the relevances of the sociological discourse, we are interpreting them as expressions of their part in the local coordination of an institutional process" (Smith 1987:190).

Smith (1987) maintains that it is important that the project never devolve into an account of relations as a system in and of itself. Although the standpoint of individuals located in their daily experience is always the point of departure, from there the researcher must explicate how institutional relations determine everyday experience and explore how invisible determination in relations generalize and are generalized. This is the method of institutional ethnography. "In contrast to such concepts as bureaucracy, 'institution' does not identify a determinate form of social organization, but rather the intersection and coordination of more than one relational mode of the ruling apparatus" (Smith 1987:160). Ethnography is not restricted to the method of observation and interviewing; rather it is a commitment to explication of how "it" really is. "Questions of validity involve reference back to those processes themselves as issues of 'does it indeed work in that way?'" (Smith 1987:160).

The standpoint approach is flexible in its application and addresses many of the shortcomings of traditional criminology; it therefore presents a method of affording youth a voice in the study of violence. As Smith (1987) indicates, the sociological strategy she has developed does not belong, or subject itself, to the interpretive procedures of any particular school of sociology. In addition, a feminist sociology is not exclusively for women; rather it approaches society and social relations from the standpoint of women situated outside the relations of ruling (Smith 1987:46). An application of this approach to youth is "constrained [only] by the project of creating a way of seeing, from where [they] actually live, into the powers, processes, and relations that organize and determine the everyday context of that seeing" (Smith 1987:9). The impact of official knowledge and relations of ruling, which affect both youth and establishment authority, will be exposed through a comparative analysis of their respective standpoints.

Although I am using Smith's theory as a basis for an alternative methodology, I am not superimposing theoretical constructs on the data. Rather than analyzing youth violence within a specific theory, my study begins with "the activities of actual individuals whose activity produces the social relations that they live" (Smith 1987:90). Smith (1987) is not suggesting that criminology can be done without knowing how to do it or that we can approach the research with a naive consciousness. Her approach challenges the implication that, because the experiences in the everyday world are unformed and unorganized, the researcher cannot enter them without a theoretical framework in which to order them.

The methods of thinking and analytic procedures of this approach must preserve the presence of the active and experiencing subject (Smith 1987:105). Although I intended to preserve the standpoint of the subjects throughout my inquiry, my method varied slightly from that of Smith. My study is a comparative, rather than integrative, analysis of the perspectives of youth and the traditional understanding of youth by establishment authority. According to Smith the interviewing should be done in two distinct stages so that, in my case, an analysis of the interviews with the youths could explicate a problematic to be specified as interview topics for the establishment authority. Although this ideal could not be realized, the process of shuttling between the two groups of respondents nonetheless proved useful, forcing me to reformulate the questionnaire to better reflect the perspectives of respondents. For example, I discussed with the youths their opinion of the programs offered to deal with violent behaviour. I presented to the establishment authorities the sentiment that anger management, for instance, was "a joke" to see how they interpreted similar programs. This reflective process, as opposed to two distinct phases of interviewing, better served my interest in a comparative analysis. Moreover, it is precisely through this comparative method that the standpoint of the youth can be achieved. In order to indicate the disjuncture between the two perspectives, it is imperative to maintain the voice and perspective of the youths' experience.

Respondents

The data for this study were derived from interviews with thirty respondents. I interviewed fourteen youth incarcerated in Willingdon Youth Detention Centre (YDC) and one youth on probation; four were girls and eleven were boys. They ranged in age from fifteen to eighteen years old. The crimes committed by the youths varied in severity. Although the violent offences were diverse, I was unable to interview any youth who had been involved in sexual offences. The senior correctional officer in charge of programming at Willingdon YDC told me that, because sex offenders were rarely housed there, none was available to speak with me. The majority of the youths had been involved in some form of assault, either inside or outside the institution. All had a prior record and most had been engaging in criminal activity since they were eight years old.

Seven of the fifteen establishment authorities interviewed were from Youth Court Services (YCS). YCS is a government institution involved in assessing youths convicted under the Young Offenders Act. Within YCS I interviewed two psychologists, three psychiatric social workers, one psychiatrist and the clinical director. I also interviewed three probation officers, two youth court judges, the local director of the "new" youth services team (Burnaby), a constable from the Vancouver city police and the officer in charge of programming (OCP) at Willingdon Detention Centre. Three of the authorities were women and twelve were men.

Youths

To better understand the perceptions of youth, it is first necessary to identify the crimes in which they were involved.

Assault was the most common offence among both the male and female youths. Two of the girls were sisters involved with another girl in an attack on a fourth. Katie,[3] the younger sister, aged fifteen, was charged with aggravated assault and uttering threats to cause death or bodily harm in an incident that was "provoked by the victim's comments." Katie's past charges included one other assault, probation breaches, possession of stolen property, possession of an illegal firearm and a break-and-enter (B&E). The victim, a former friend of the older sister, Tara, "had said some untrue things" about Katie, with whom she did not get along. Katie explained:

> Because she said, "I'm going to kick your ass," I take that as saying "Let's fight" so I'm like "Oh I'd like to see you try," so we went up to the park. My friend jumped on her [and] it got past the point of being a fight and became like a beating I guess.

A doctor testified that if the victim had received one more kick, she would have died. Although she did not remember saying it to the victim, Katie explained to me that the threats charge was in reference to her commenting that she would do something to the victim if she told the police. Tara was also briefly involved, which is, according to both girls, very much out of character for her. During the fight, Tara explained that she picked up the girl who was being beaten.

> I said, "Have you had enough? Say you've had enough and she'll stop hitting you" and she said, "No" and she spit at me, and when she spit it was bloody and so I picked her up and I hit her and I threw her on the ground and walked away.

Andrea, another female offender, had a lengthy history of offences, including assault with a weapon causing harm, stalking and intimidation, harassment and being unlawfully at large. The crime we spoke most about was her assault on a girl who had "ratted out" Andrea's best friend. As Andrea explained: "I didn't want any evidence so I tortured her mentally kind of thing." She also stated that it got worse after she had consumed alcohol. "Then I was like fuck, oh I hate you and I beat her up some more. They said I had a knife and I cut her but I don't think I did; maybe I slipped when I was drunk." At the end of the interview Andrea indicated: "I'm not really doing time for a violent offence right now; I'm doing time for an AWOL and for trying to rob some chick because I was high."

Other youths who had committed assault included seventeen-year-old Mark, who, along with his brother, attacked their mother's boyfriend with ski poles. The reason, Mark explained, "was because he owed my mom rent money, … he was hitting my mom, … and I found these court papers that said he was a convicted child molester." Mark was released on bail for that charge and is currently in Willingdon for an additional assault in which he claimed: "I just got drunk and flipped out on my friend." A serious assault was committed by another male offender, Ron:

> Me and a couple of my friends went to a party one night on an Indian reserve, so it was a Native party. We were the only five White guys there. A little feud started between me and about fifteen other guys, so I just got mad and started smashing them all.

In describing the victim's injuries, Ron indicated: "I smashed his head in with a bumper-jack and gave him a compound fracture to his skull." Ron explained that they were all drinking, "which contributed in a big way."

All three of the youths were charged, one for attempted vehicular manslaughter "because he ran someone over."

Alex was a Native youth described as having "aggression problems" both in and out of jail, which was partially the result of his suffering from fetal alcohol syndrome. He made no reference to this characterization. Alex had a series of assault and robbery charges and, as the OCP commented, "Social services gave up trying to help him." Alex explained that he had lived in foster homes but "they didn't work out [because] they treat people like dirt." When I asked what he had done he explained: "I just go around with my friends and beat people; I don't know why." The most recent arrest was for assault and robbery of someone who had "ratted [his] friend out."

Like so many others, Garth explained that a lot of his crimes were related to needing money. "I had just got out [of jail], was on crack and I needed money, so I just started doing crime, ... breaking into houses and stuff." His record included two B&Es, dangerous driving, two possession of stolen property charges, breaches, warrants and one assault charge. Garth claimed that many of his problems started when he was eight years old and was sexually abused by his mom's boyfriend. "I was mad at the cops because they never put the guy in jail because he beat one of those lie-detector tests." Similarly, Clint broke into a school and stole items like televisions and VCRs because, as he explains, "I came out of jail from the last sentence and had no place to go. I stole this stuff so I could get through the week." Ed was on probation at the time of the interview and had been involved in an armed robbery with three other people because, as he said, "We needed some money at the time." Ed was on the "look out" while he and his friends walked into a store with a few machetes and a pocket knife and "held up" the cashier. No one was hurt during the incident so the youth did not consider it a violent offence.

Other crimes motivated by a need for money included those of Graham, a youth who had recently returned to Willingdon on a mischief charge. He had "done time" both in YDC and in adult prison for robbery and assault. Graham's latest arrest occurred after the police found his fingerprints on a car he had stolen three years earlier. Graham's previous robbery charge stemmed from when, he explained, "Me and my buddy had no money so we walked into a mall parking lot, we saw two kids and we pulled a knife on them and said, 'Give us your money.'" Josh was charged with extortion, which "is sort of like blackmail I guess; asking people for money and, if they don't give it, you threaten them." Josh and his co-accused requested $800 and told the victim, "If you don't give it, we're going to shoot you." He explained a previous extortion charge: "[It] was the same thing but more severe. We kicked down the door, ran into the house, beat him up, beat up the little brother and trashed the house.

We did it because my friend gave him a stereo and stuff and he didn't pay."

Daryl was most recently in prison for what he stated was "minor stuff": possession of stolen property, a couple of B&Es and a high-speed chase. When he was thirteen he broke out of jail in the Northwest Territories; while at large, he and another escaped inmate broke into a house, stole some guns and hid there. Meanwhile the owner came home and, Daryl claimed, "We didn't know what to do so we said we were taking him with us." They put a gun to his head and made the man drive with them in his car. When they stopped for gas the man told the cashier to phone the police and the two youths escaped on foot and were eventually caught across town. Daryl's co-accused started fighting with the police, and Daryl escaped and hid in the bushes. He later broke into an abandoned house from which, he explained, "I grabbed a towel rack, walked to the neighbour's house, rang the door bell, and whoever answered the door I smacked them and walked away." When I asked Daryl why he did that, he said, "I don't know why; it was right after the confinement happened [and] my head was just racing. I didn't know what was going on, where I was, just too much stuff happened at once." He was charged with assault with a weapon and unlawful confinement.

I also interviewed three youths who had been charged with murder. Dave explained his experience:

> Me and five other guys were going to rob this guy and we beat the shit out of him and he died in his sleep. We just wanted the cash but he wouldn't give it up, so we pounded him; he was an easy target because he was intoxicated.

The charge was reduced to manslaughter because, as the youth recalled, "I had no intention [of killing him]; none of us did." The young man is currently awaiting trial in adult court. Todd was charged with stabbing to death a seventy-year-old man but claims he did not take part in the actual act.

> I met a kid at a job two days before it happened. We started doing a bunch of drugs, and then this one night we were driving home from a party and he pulled over, broke into someone's house and killed him.... I thought it was just going to be a B&E. I didn't help with the murder but I was there when it happened and I didn't do anything to stop it and I didn't go to the cops afterwards, so I was charged.

Finally, I interviewed Jane, who was charged with second-degree murder after assisting in the killing of her pimp: "I got involved when I was fourteen with a prostitution ring and I couldn't get out because of my pimp; my life was on the line." Jane explained that she did not know if she was more scared of the other girls or of the pimp because both had threatened to kill her. Jane paused several times throughout her description of what had happened: "This is hard for me; I really want to explain to you how it was but it's hard." Jane was drinking in the woods with her two co-accused, who were older and had planned the crime. She described her co-accused as tough, Hispanic gang members. "I didn't really know what was happening. At the time [one of my co-accused] said she was going to give him the money that she owed him." When he arrived the three girls beat the pimp and drowned him in the nearby creek. "I fell in love with this guy.... I degraded myself and I couldn't take it anymore. I was too involved. I never intended to hurt anybody, 'cause that's not who I am." This interview was particularly hard, not only because it was difficult for her to talk about these events, but also because of the stark contrast between what she was telling me and the fact that she was eating ice-cream like an average sixteen-year-old. Jane's other charges included theft under $1000 and possession of a deadly weapon. She explained the latter incident: "I was twelve and my mom used to beat me and one night she came after me and I picked up a knife. I just grabbed it because I was scared; I was tired of it."

Establishment Authority

It is important to detail the position and responsibilities of each establishment authority to glean a better idea of their contact and experience with violent youth.[4]

One of the psychologists at YDC explained that, as part of the assessment process, their team is responsible for predisposition reports, to give the judges an indication of fitness to stand trial; assessment of the offenders' needs, problems and appropriate sentences; and recommendations to raise to adult court cases of serious youth crime. Psychologists, social workers and nurses administer treatment for sex offenders through individual counselling and group therapy; and psychologists and psychiatric social workers conduct anger management sessions and other forms of one-to-one counselling. The psychiatrist interviewed was also involved in assessment, treatment, follow-up procedures, clinicals for sexual offenders and response to the problems of youths while in Willingdon. The director of YCS participates in and oversees these procedures and was attempting to expand anger management to a multisystem approach.

The authorities at YCS have contact with the youths in two places. First contact occurs in the out-patient department, where the authorities do psychological assessment, including intellectual, personality and projective testing. The youths are interviewed by a team of psychologists, psychiatrists and social workers, who write the report that is submitted to the court. One of the psychiatric social workers indicated that their specific job was to provide the background, or social history, of the offender through speaking with the people, such as parents, teachers and probation officers, who have the most contact with the child. The second site of authority–youth contact is the in-patient department, where youths are observed for two weeks, twenty-four hours a day, "under a little more natural situation." They undergo a battery of psychological tests and are questioned about their behaviour.

I also interviewed three probation officers. One was the acting supervisor of the specialized probation unit, which "deals with the most violent young offenders and street youth that we think are in need of intense supervision, which is defined not only by the criminal activity but the lifestyle they lead." Another probation officer interviewed had been part of the specialized unit but was transferred following the amalgamation of five ministries—Social Services, the Attorney General, Education, Health and Women's Equality—into the Ministry of Children and Families to ensure a "continuity in service when it comes to issues like attending court, writing reports for judges and supervising offenders in the community." The third youth probation officer described herself as "an officer of the court first and foremost: a neutral third party that's in the court room." She explained that her position "also entails seeing clients, a lot of networking and liaisons with group homes, defence/ Crown counsel—all the contractors that are involved, such as one-to-one workers from the Public Legal Education Association (PLEA), group-home workers and family counsellors. I deal with kids on bail, probation and conditional release; and every kid in custody has a youth worker attached to them.... I'm involved in their release planning." She also writes diversional reports, pre-disposition reports, and raised hearing reports.[5]

I interviewed two youth court judges, one of whom made "off-the-record" comments over the telephone and asked not to be quoted. The second judge was conducting a provincial inquiry into the services for children and youth and recommending the amalgamation of the five separate ministries. He referred me to the former head of corrections in the probation office in Burnaby who is now the local director of the new youth services team. He is referred to as the "team leader" in the youth services office and is responsible for designing and administering the model for the newly created ministry.

The detective constable for the youth services section of the Vancouver city police was another respondent. Prior to interviewing the constable I viewed an episode of a local television program entitled *Crime, Prevention and You*, on which he discussed the topic, "Youth at Risk." He stated that the need for the specialized unit was realized in 1992: "We were finding more and more incidents of youth crime, so we downsized the gang squad because we found that the gangs involved a lot of youth [rather than] typical gangs like Los Leabos, which are much more structured and removed from the street." He described his current position as "getting involved in lengthy investigations ... from the initial crime, through charges and follow-up in any offences involving youth."

Finally, I interviewed the senior correctional officer in charge of programs (OCP) at Willingdon, who helped me to arrange the interviews with the youths. It is her responsibility to orient new youths, assess their needs, determine their length of stay and enrol them in rehabilitative programs. She added, "I also classify internally which means really getting to know the kids, the way they behave and how they function." In addition, she is co-facilitator of "The Keys to Excellence Program," through which the youths work on setting goals and recognizing and changing behaviours.

It became apparent during the first interviews that some of my questions were too broad; the respondents could not generalize on certain issues. For instance, when asked "Are there common characteristics among the youths who commit violent acts?" several establishment authorities stated that they could not give general descriptions. One of the judges explained that "the trouble with the question and any answer is it's all relative; yes we see more Chinese teenagers committing acts of violence, but we have a much larger Chinese community." One of the psychologists said that the youths cut across all ethnic and socio-economic backgrounds. As one social psychiatric worker indicated, "It's not just poor kids; that was never really the case. Maybe half come from the middle or upper classes."

Conclusion

Dorothy Smith recognizes that a critique is more than a negative statement; it is an attempt to define an alternative (1987:78). Through assessing the problems in many traditional approaches, Smith and others (for example, Cain 1990; James and Prout 1990; James 1993; James and Jenks 1996) have developed a fresh alternative for data collection. A real advantage to the standpoint approach is that it can be extended beyond the study of women to other silenced groups, such as young people. This is not to deny the obvious difficulty in transporting a method designed for adults to a cohort of young people; but still the core idea of incorporating the voice of absent subjects into a topic that concerns them remains the objective. Violent youths are typically ignored not only because they offend societal perceptions of what constitutes a child, but also because of the age-old belief that criminals, by the nature of their actions, do not have a right to be heard.

By advocating an approach that recognizes the importance of uncovering and preserving the standpoint of young offenders, in no way do I mean to belittle the devastating consequences of youth violence. Furthermore, I am not suggesting that young people should be afforded the responsibility and decision-making power of adults. However, as indicated throughout this chapter, we need a method that allows for greater awareness of, and an ability to listen to, what youth offenders have to say. The benefits are reciprocal: the voice of youth would contribute to knowledge about youth violence by providing a new perspective; and young offenders, who perhaps more than anyone else lack self-worth, would know that their opinion is valued and instructive. By comparing their perspective to that of establishment authority, it may be possible to identify the dysfunction in understanding the problem. This disjuncture will be highlighted and analyzed in the next two chapters.

Notes

1. In an article addressing critiques of her work, Smith explains that the notion of "standpoint" has been transformed from the original intent. She states that she and others used the notion of "women's standpoint" to express a particular phase of the women's movement, one which recognized women as speaking, knowing subjects in the experience of women. The concept of "standpoint" has been formalized through feminist theorizing. Although inevitable, formalization "breaks connection with the original experience that sought expression in a variety of terms ... it displaces the practical politics that the notion 'standpoint' originally captured ... it is reduced to a purely discursive function" (Smith 1992:89). Hence, the notion of standpoint does not stand alone as a theoretical construct but rather is a place where inquiry begins (Smith 1992:91).

2. In 1952 the American Psychiatric Association published the first edition of the *Diagnostic and Statistical Manual of Mental Disorders* (DSM). The DSM provides descriptions of various disorders, from which clinicians select the appropriate diagnoses. The DSM has undergone several revisions and has become the classification system most widely used in North America (Smith 1993:500). The most current revision is the DSM-IV (1994), which includes the "multiaxial classification" through which "each individual is to be rated on five separate dimensions, or axes ... forc[ing] the diagnostician to consider a broad range of information" (Davison and Neale 1994:60).

3. All of the names have been changed. A brief biography of each youth respondent can be found in Appendix I.

4. A summary of the establishment authorities and their affiliation with the youths is found in Appendix II.
5. Diversion reports acknowledge that some young offenders should not be subjected to formal youth court sanctions but instead "diverted" from the system. These reports outline why a youth should be given "alternative measures," such as writing an essay related to the offence or doing community service work, which is the type of formal diversion authorized by the Young Offenders Act (Corrado et al. 1992:367).

Pre-disposition reports assist a youth court judge in deciding what "disposition"—distinct from a sentence, which is reserved for adults—to impose on a convicted young offender (Corrado et al. 1992:368). These reports are usually prepared by a probation officer or youth court worker who is familiar with the background and circumstances of the offender.

Raised hearing reports are prepared for the hearing in youth court to determine if a young person charged with a very serious offence may be "raised" to the adult court for trial and, if convicted, sentenced there (Corrado et al. 1992:370). These reports include recommendations for or against the transfer to adult count based on the age and record of the offender and the severity of the offence.

Chapter Three

Disjuncture in Comprehending and Portraying Youths

From the outset of this study I have employed the term "establishment authority" to describe the publicly and professionally recognized experts in the field of youth justice and violent youth. I acknowledge, however, that their knowledge does not incorporate the perspective of those of whom they speak. Hence, while they are authorities within their profession, their expertise is not a function of the personal experience of violent offenders. This was particularly evident during the interview process. As Todd stated: "I don't know why they call themselves 'experts' because they've never done it; they don't know what it's like and they've never bothered to ask me."

The interviews also reveal how establishment authorities are part of what Smith (1987) describes as the "ruling apparatus." Although the ruling apparatus comprises the total complex of powerful institutions, the people involved in the youth justice system can be seen as one element, which supports the relations of ruling. They are adult authorities who participate in a hierarchical, power-based correctional system that has complete control over offenders' lives. The rationale for the programming and treatment of violent youths is based on "professional" analyses, which conform to standards established through other relations of ruling. Hence, establishment authority is sometimes supportive of change and reform but not to the extent of overthrowing or even challenging existing relations of ruling. Establishment authorities are part of the status quo and both explicitly and implicitly seek to maintain the existing ruling apparatus as the most effective and efficient way of "knowing." This knowledge is perpetuated by the standards of other authorities, such as government and academia. The ruling apparatus itself is dependent upon social relations that enforce the silence of those subjected to authority.

Children or adolescents are subjugated by all relations of ruling throughout each stage of the criminal justice system once they have been apprehended for a violent offence. After the crime, the collective weight and "wisdom" of officialdom are superimposed on the accumulated consciousness of the youths, often in a purposeful attempt to negate their own perspective. Youths, who are powerless in terms of their perceived knowledge and status, are told by the powerful that what they have done is wrong, regardless of how they themselves feel. Thus, the youths' experience is often at variance with the matrix of social relations derived from the ruling apparatus. In fact, the responses in the interviews supported James' and Jenks' (1996) recognition that, even when youths are asked their opinion, their words are viewed by adults with either suspicion or indifference. Establishment authority often appears interested in listening to youths' perspectives only when those views reproduce the social relations upon which the ruling apparatus is based.

In essence, the definition and deviant attributes of youth crime have been imposed on society generally and youth in particular. The extent to which youths embody or resist such definition is not recognized by the authorities. Because youths are excluded from the production of knowledge on the issue of youth violence, their ways of knowing are not represented either in the public discourse or in the institutions through which they are incarcerated. Their views are further masked by the false assumption of authorities that youths naturally aspire to societal goals (James 1993; Acland 1995), an assumption underscored by the programs offered. The process is compounded by what Smith (1987) describes as a "bifurcation of consciousness" among those who are silenced. On the one hand, youths have their own ways of knowing based on personal experience; on the other, the institutional context in which they live dilute, if not subvert, their own understanding in favour of the goals and ideology imposed by the justice system. Although they are not always aware of it, youths' ways of thinking are "authorized," if not presupposed, by external sources. Nowhere was this more evident than in the system of rewards at Willingdon. This clearly supports James' (1993) notion that adult theories directly infringe upon and pre-empt the real-life experiences of youths. In fact, the very operation of the youth justice system, as presently constituted, is premised on, and is a function of, social relations geared to the silencing of youths.

Thus, as will be illustrated below, there is a definite disjuncture between the youth violence perspective of young offenders and that of establishment authority. However, because this study intends to discuss the "extent" of the disjuncture, the discussion must also include areas of agreement between the two groups of respondents. It is neither practical nor useful to include two hundred pages of transcribed "voices" from the respondent interviews, although it is possible to identify four discrete issues that emerge from the data. The first two, which inform the content of this chapter, are the pathologization of violent youth and the inaccurate and sensationalized media representations of the young offender, especially the violent girl. The last two issues, how the youth justice system works and the means to improve it, are discussed in Chapter Four.

The first section of this chapter examines how violent youths have become "folk devils," to whom are attributed characteristics that feed societal panic but clash with the youths' perceptions of self. Youths are pathologized within professional discourse and portrayed as unremorseful monsters in need of medical treatment. Explaining youth crime as an individual problem denies the structural and cultural barriers that youths say contribute to their actions. These professional stereotypes are reproduced and confirmed as "truths" through such powerful institutions as the media. An analysis of these truths forms the basis of the second section of this chapter, which focuses on a CBC documentary shaped by "expert" knowledge on violent females. Several of my respondents were interviewed in the film but were critical of how they were portrayed. This invokes an analysis of the wider purpose of the media and their connection to the ruling apparatus. Conversely, the extent to which "experts" use movies as explanations for violence is also an important element shaping the perception of both establishment authorities and youths. Overall, it is obvious that the perceptions of the two groups conflict because the youths' opinions of, and experiences with, violence are either ignored or reinterpreted in professional and popular discourse.

Understanding the Violent Youth

Although the premise of this study is that youths' voices are not included in the understanding of youth violence, there are two occasions when youths are asked their opinion. Non-offending youths are interviewed on the street or at school to get their opinion for the local news; and young offenders at various stages in the justice system are interviewed by officials to glean an understanding of the circumstances surrounding the commission of crime. Still, such information is often manipulated to support professional discourse. The voices of youth are dressed in professional jargon and concepts alien to the young person's experience. This is illustrated in issues pertaining to biomedical categorization, remorse, individual explanations of violence and stereotyping.

Medicalization and Classification of Violent Youths
To present a comparative analysis of perceptions among respondents, it is important to first establish the public view and "official" understanding of violent youth. Drawing on Cohen (1980) and Schissel (1997), it is

evident that violent youths have become a particularly visible social category of "folk devil." Schissel (1997:30) explains:

> [F]olk devils are inherently deviant and are presumed to be self-seeking, out of control and in danger of undermining stability of society.... [They] are constructed in the context of moral panic and are imbued with stereotypical characteristics that set them apart from normal, law-abiding society, making it easy for average citizens to become embroiled in the alarm over crime and to call for harsh justice.

In keeping with the notion of "folk devils," Giroux (1996) uses the term "fugitive cultures" to explain how youth as a social construction has become indeterminant, alien and sometimes hazardous in the public eye. A source of repeated moral panics and the object of social regulation, youth cannot be contained and controlled within a limited number of social spheres (Giroux 1996:11). Acland (1995), too, is concerned with the way in which criminalized youth has become Other, distant yet inseparable from the social order. Citing Stallybrass and White (1986), Acland claims that such demarcations are always dependent upon disgust and desire (Acland 1995:19).

The mainstream characterizations of violent youths reflect the position of the professionals describing them. Increasingly, the "biomedical" (Conrad and Schneider 1980) understanding of crime has defined criminal actions in terms of illness, shifting the definition of criminality from bad to sick behaviour. "Crime, rather than being primarily an issue of morality or politics, becomes a problem to be solved by applying the allegedly neutral technology of medical practice" (Kelly 1992:172).

The emphasis on the medical model as an explanatory framework for crime and the domination of psychologists and psychiatrists in youth institutions has resulted in the pathologizing of violent youth. This is evident in how the youths are characterized in their files by Youth Court Services. The psychological assessment in Andrea's file says she is "a conduct-disorder girl who has all the earmarks of an early borderline personality disorder ... [and who] needs a good deal of monitoring in the future in an attempt to sort out the particular aspect of her mood that put her at risk for future mental disorders." In defence of the profession, one of the psychologists explained: "We talk about the risk of sex offenders and risk in terms of being raised [to adult] ... but we don't specifically label kids high-risk for violence unless requested." In contrast to the information in the files, the psychologist further commented, "I never use the term 'violent offender' or try and label people that way or put them into categories." The youths, however, indicated that categories were imposed on them, although they resisted such classification. Katie explained:

> You go to Youth Court Services and they label you, they give you
> the meds and you probably don't need that label and there is
> probably a more reasonable explanation and you're stuck with
> the label. They tried to put me on medication but I don't think I
> need them. I know a lot of my friends are addicted to Prozac and
> Ritalin and they think they can't do without it and I tell them,
> "Yes you can. You can probably do better without it."

Andrea, who had tied up her assault victim, said, "They wrote this big assessment on how I have problems and the psychiatrist said I was sadomasochistic."

Although the authorities conduct extensive interviews with youths for social history reports, predisposition reports and psychological assessments, at no point do they consider what the youths tell them as valuable in its own right. Rather, this information is interpreted to reaffirm professional discourse. For example, one psychologist explained that they are able to assess interviewees using the Psychopathy Checklist[1] (PCL) (Hare 1993), to determine if they are psychopaths. Another authority commented:

> Violent offenders almost inevitably have some marked psychiatric problem. And we need to recognize that some have a very low
> intellect; their IQ is at such a low point that many of the programs / approaches we've taken in the past are very ineffective.

In essence, establishment authority interprets youths' opinions or behaviour through a specialized language, which pathologizes the experience of youth. As James and Jenks (1996) argue, children are not given any authority over the interpretation of their experience and thus are not part of "redefinition."

In addition to pathologizing and medicalizing youths, authorities create classifications that mystify the understanding of youth violence because the typologies are foreign to youths' experience. For example, to comprehend the "violent youth," some of the authorities at Youth Court Services said I should narrow my focus to one kind of violence. As was explained, there are two kinds of violence; the first is "instrumental aggression," whereby there is a purpose to the violence. It involves experiential learning and "often includes dysfunctional perceptions that justify violence as a means to an end." This is the type of violence employed by gangs and psychopaths. According to cognitive theorists in

Abnormal Psychology, "certain schemata and irrational interpretations are factors in abnormality" (Davison and Neale 1994:56). The second type of violence, as was explained by Youth Court Services authorities, is "reactive aggression," which is done out of anger or frustration in responding to the perception of threat. "It is reflective of beliefs about appropriate behaviour, roles and values."

By comparison, the youths made no reference to these types of violence. Most often youths' definition of violence had to do with simply hurting someone, but rarely, no matter how severe the assault, did they view themselves as inherently violent. Several youths made a clear distinction between themselves as people and the act of violence. For example, Tara stated: "What I did was violent but I hate to think of it like that because I can't think of myself as a violent person, but I hit somebody. I think you can commit a violent act but not be a violent person." Ron said that he considered himself a violent person only when he was fighting. Hence, the classification of the young respondents as "violent youth" by the authorities, and admittedly by me, is an inaccurate description of who they are. This categorization totalizes youths: violence becomes the sole characteristic of their being. As Daryl stated: "When I went to court they judged my whole life, my whole personality just on one incident. They didn't mention that I play on an all-star hockey team, that I help with retarded kids at school. I've been good my whole life and then I did this one little thing and they base their whole report just on that." Although Dave beat a man to death he said: "I don't want to be violent, and I don't want people to be scared of me; I'm not a monster, I can be a nice guy, a caring person."

Unremorseful Monsters

Painting violent youths as monsters makes it difficult for establishment authority to see youths as capable of remorse. And yet remorse is a central feature of the official assessment of criminality. All of the establishment authorities agree that "distress or internal discomfort" on the part of the offender are an indication of remorse and hence a measure of the potential for the individual not to reoffend in the future. As one psychologist explained, remorse is a crucial issue when dealing with murderers, because, in keeping with provisions of the YOA, it is factored into the decision of raising youths to adult court.

In theory, remorse is an objective index of both the extent to which offenders have become contrite and, subsequently, their readiness for reintegration into normal and polite society. In practice, remorse is a religiously and socially sanctioned mechanism through which authorities are allowed to label and pathologize youths who do not conform in ways deemed necessary. Operationally, the concept of remorse individualizes and psychologizes youth crime by blaming youth offenders for their mistakes, allowing authorities to ignore poverty and other structural factors that contextualize individual behaviour. The oppressive nature of these processes is particularly underscored in the relationship between the concepts of remorse and abnormality, a term which is used as a weapon against those who defy the expected.

> To confess is to admit to a form of deviance, and not to demonstrate remorse is to risk being labelled a sociopath. In this respect, the confessor must "want" to confess and must "display" remorse to fully "return to the social." (Acland 1995:89)

As part of their repentance, offenders are expected to address the gap between deviance and normalcy. This is accomplished through what Hepworth and Turner (1982) call "moral gateways," which include the legal pardon, "paying one's debt to society," mercy and the confession (Hepworth and Turner 1982 cited in Acland 1995:87). These gateways are considered rituals of "social inclusion" because they permit the reorientation of the deviant into the consensual moral and social structure. Expressions of remorse, such as the confession, also operate ideologically to legitimize the moral order and the legal force wielded by authorities. Hence, remorse is seen as an act of communication that confirms the existence of a shared societal view of what is right and wrong.

For Foucault (1979), however, the confession is not a one-directional moral gateway, but an expression of "power/knowledge." Confessions and remorse are accepted or rejected based on the explicit authority of those who hear and witness them (Acland 1995:88). In essence, confession and remorse are linked to authority and power relations—specifically the "authority to hear" and to interpret the information without consideration of the original speaker (Acland 1995:88).

The justice system uses psychological testing to measure the youths' capacity for remorse. The psychiatrist explained, "We don't ask [if the youths are remorseful] straight out, but we ask what they did the night after, how they slept, what did they think the victim's family feels." Their responses are interpreted by using the Psychopathy Checklist (PCL); according to the psychiatrist, "some youths fit the pattern of having little ability to empathize, lack of feelings for others [and] little emotional reaction. Others have severe reactions. We found that those with high PCL scores are more likely to commit violent crimes."

The authorities explained that youths express three degrees of remorse; they appear to echo Kohlberg's moral development theory (1969). In the first degree of remorse youths feel badly because they got caught and their freedom is restricted. A probation officer explained, "In some cases they feel frustrated and are not quite sure why they did it and are not aware of the consequences until after the fact." In the second degree of remorse youths feel ashamed, and they understand that what they did was wrong. Several authorities stated that this type of remorse is very rare. In the third degree of remorse youths do not have any remorse, feel no responsibility and do not care. The authorities said that this was the most common reaction among youths: "Very few feel remorse about anything; they are so self-centred."

The supposed objectivity of measuring degrees of remorse was proven false by the authorities' assertion that few violent youths are truly remorseful. Most authorities commented that, even when youths expressed remorse, they often lack true sentiment. The psychiatrist stated,

> I feel that if somebody expresses remorse verbally that means nothing to me; if they express nothing that means the person is really bad. On the other hand, some kids show symptoms such as depression and inability to sleep following a criminal act, [and] that reflects true remorse.... After being in YDC for two months, I don't believe what they say because they learn very quickly. With exposure to programs, court, lawyers, they are prompted to recognize remorse as a central issue. They give lip service to it without understanding what it means.

The authorities' tendency to mistrust most expressions of remorse contrasts with the voice of youth. In explaining her reaction to the fight Tara said:

> I feel bad that [the victim] got hurt as much as she did. I don't think anyone deserves to get beaten up that bad, no matter what they've done. I feel worse about what it did to her family. I just reverse that on myself and I would hate the person that put my family in that situation. It affected so many people.

The common adult belief that young offenders lack respect for anyone but themselves is contradicted by the majority of the youths, who spoke with great admiration for their families and who felt a particular need to protect younger siblings. For example, Katie remarked, "I didn't want to fight at my mom's house in case she came home; it's my mom's property [and] I respect her." Tara was concerned about her youngest sister witnessing the assault: "I didn't want her to see that. I realized 'oh God there's a little kid here,' so I yelled at them to stop." Others commented that they were trying to prevent their siblings from ending up in jail and that the guilt of hurting their parents was one reason to abandon crime. Josh said, "My family is worried about me. I think it's good because they haven't given up on me yet.... I probably won't do any more crime, I just don't want to hurt my parents." It is interesting that, while the discourse on youth violence often pleads for including the moral responsibility of youths in the analysis of crime, it never recognizes that some incarcerated youths do take responsibility for their crimes (see Barkley 1998).

The authorities' inability or unwillingness to perceive remorse indicates their failure to contextualize youth violence. Several youths acknowledged that what they had done was wrong by the authorities' standards, but not necessarily by their own. Mark said, "The [victims] deserved it but it's my fault. They screwed me around, so I beat the shit out of them. I could have got around that, but *I did what made sense to me*" (italics added). In such cases, the authorities' simplistic insistence on an expression of remorse ignores the violent context of youths' experience and their limited means of dealing with real-life situations on the street. This lack of contextualization is reflected in the diagnostic and behaviour classifications applied by the authorities to violent youth. As Kelly (1992:69) recognizes, these categories reveal nothing about the youths themselves but speak more to the relations and process whereby the professionals construct their classifications, and apply and justify them.

The above suggests that the significance placed on remorse is more a reflection of the power relations between the authorities and the youths, the ideology associated with the medical model and the need to reproduce social order, than it is a measure of criminality. As with the confession, remorse is an ideologically laden instrument to defend conformity. The characterization of violent youths as remorseless monsters is compounded by professional stereotypes that feed the current moral panic. One distorted image, which harkens back to notions of intrinsic childhood evil, stresses the ever-descending age of violent youth. Several authorities commented that presently "young murderers seem to get younger" (Acland 1995:5). The OCP said that she notices youth starting violent crime at a much earlier age than before: "It used to be a progression that was easy to see. I get really shocked at the level of violence of kids at age 13–14; that is really different."

Another misconception adopted by authorities is that most violent youth are members of a gang, "a word [that] is never defined but is used loosely to refer to kids who 'hang around' in twos or threes and have an identifiable ethnicity or class" (Schissel 1997:58). Gangs are perceived to be so pervasive that, as the detective constable explained, police departments have established entire units to deal with the problem. Youth crime is often racialized by authorities who commonly attribute its most violent forms to ethnically-based gangs. One probation officer explained that "a lot of Asian, Vietnamese and Indo-Canadian gangs are carrying high-powered weapons, and that puts a whole different slant on youth gangs." Contradicting such images, however, are the views of youths themselves. Several youth respondents took exception to authorities associating them with a gang. Tara was one of them: "In my file from the police where it says gang-affiliated it says 'yes,' but I've never been involved in a gang." In a typical scenario, the effect of such a classification became apparent in her later experiences with the justice system:

> The prosecution made me sound really bad, like I was the big horrible gang member. He called me vicious about five times, which shocked me to the core because I am anything but vicious. And they described me as cold on the stand, but I cried on the stand so I don't know why that was said.

The emphasis on Other and the supposed development of a new breed of kids are both sparking fear and hatred among the public. As Acland explains:

> The crimes themselves do not speak their reason; that is the function of the broader social apparatus. As something becomes part of cultural knowledge, or even a certain popular cultural "literacy," a whole referencial and significatory fabric of forces moves as well. (1995:11)

For example, Davis (1988) points out how the crisis of gang violence in Los Angeles operates with respect to the order of racial, ageist and class struggle (cited in Acland 1995:11). The moral panic concerning youth has become so pervasive that, as Acland argues, youth violence is now part of our "common sense": "It is suffused throughout civil society and, importantly, has become central in the structuring of a particular moment of hegemony" (1995:143).

Overall, it is evident that the authorities attempt to judge the criminality of youths by their degree of remorse and by other stereotypes. It should not be surprising, then, that several youths have learned to deny their subjectivity and express themselves in accordance with professional discourse. Ironically one psychologist commented that "objectification of people is very much an egocentric part of the problem. The kids are doing things to meet their own needs/wants and [they have] a twisted sense of reality." The youths who choose to express their reality run the risk of being pathologized. In several cases the youths clearly stated that they understand that what they did was wrong by society's standards, but they often defended their actions based on their own reality. For example,

Jane said that she is responsible for the murder of her pimp, even though her co-accused were more in charge of the situation. "It doesn't matter what he did, he didn't take my life ... and I can't blame [my co-accused]. I can only take responsibility for myself, and I do." Later on in the interview Jane also indicated that the murder provided a feeling of release. "It set me free, even though I'm in jail, I'm free. If it hadn't happened, I'd still probably be in prostitution, still with those girls, and doing drugs."

Individual versus Structural Explanations of Violence

The importance attributed to the medical model and the consequent need to classify behaviour have blindly focused the authorities' attention on individual explanations of violence, thereby ignoring the structural realities that govern the lives of youth. As Schissel explains, in official discourse "the ways of speaking about young offenders are restricted largely to individual or family-based accounts of the origins of crime. Rarely are the explanations based on structural inequalities or the injustices people suffer while living on the margins of society" (1997:105). By comparison, the youths themselves readily contextualized their behaviour by pointing to structural factors, often associated with their socioeconomic position in society. Poverty, early victimization and a need for respect all figured as experience-based explanations of their violent actions. However, in the collective mind of authorities, these structural determinants were either misinterpreted or conspicuously unacknowledged.

The age-old connection between poverty and crime takes on a new twist when it is applied to youths in the present economic climate. Acland explains:

> The rising market power of youth as consumers of culture [means] that youth [have] achieved a certain conspicuous position in popular culture. This involved the abundant visibility of the movements and desires of an entire generation as well as the spectacle of purchasing power and lifestyle consumption. (Acland 1995:137)

The media in particular present the connection between self-worth and designer clothes, expensive cars and sex appeal, as discussed in the next section. In essence, youths are bombarded with unattainable images of who they should be and what they should have, but these images are incongruent with the bitter realities of youth unemployment. "More youth have increasingly more idle time, and the work that is available is poorly paid, bereft of benefits, and offers little in terms of meaningful apprenticeship" (Schissel 1997:11). Although these economic barriers were not recognized by the authorities, several youths commented that much of their crime was motivated by lack of money.

Race is also at issue in the perceived increase in youth violence. By focusing on individual explanations of crime, authorities overlook cultural and language barriers, as well as the destructive impact of racism, when assessing the behaviour of immigrant and racialized youths. But the salience of race and racial barriers is recognized by youth minorities themselves. Ed, who is Chinese, commented, "The people I hang around with are Vietnamese people. They come from a tough country and, when they come here, they're mostly on their own." He explained the situation of one of his friends whose mother was left with small children and who now commits crime to pay for their food and clothing. However, the importance of culture and poverty are ignored by those who oversee the youth justice system. One of the probation officers claimed that "there is a different breed of kids, [namely] Vietnamese youths, who have come over during war-torn periods and have been exposed and sensitized to a different level of violence." On the surface, such a statement implies an understanding of culture-specific factors but, in reality, it pathologizes a particular immigrant group. Schissel (1997:58–71) addresses the connection made between violence and racialized or immigrant groups in popular culture. As Ed observed, "Most cops here are racist; down in Surrey if they see an Asian walking alone with a group down the street, they'll pull you over and question you. If you're Asian, they assume you're part of a gang."

Professional discourse reports that those who offend most often have experienced some form of familial violence growing up. A psychiatric social worker stated that "[v]iolence is learned; the most violent kids come from violent backgrounds either from parents or siblings." As the psychiatrist explained, "There are certain things always present in these kids. The most important in my opinion is abandonment and neglect by parents/caregivers, then other abuses such as physical and sexual." He also said that there is rarely stability in their homes; even when there are two parents, they are doing other things that result in emotional neglect of the children.

However, from the perspective of youths, neglect was not as important as the authorities judged, nor was violence—as pervasive as it was—always recognized as such. Interestingly, in the case of the two sisters, Katie, who was accused of being more violent, saw her family as being violent, while Tara did not. Katie explained that her family members were all bikers:

I grew up seeing people get beat up all the time [but] I was never abused; my mom would never hit me. But this one guy was bothering me once when I was six and my mom got his legs broken and that's like normal … it's part of life.

Although Katie did not give any indication of being sexually abused, according to her file she had been molested as a young child. Tara, however, had a slightly different opinion of growing up: "Maybe somebody else would describe it as violent but I don't think I would. I did see people fight, but I don't know that it affected me really deeply." Alex told me that he had a good family life growing up. However, when I asked how his mother reacted to the crimes he had committed, he told me that, at that time, she had been in jail for shoplifting in order to support her drug habit.

Like officials, the youths were cognizant that family and home environment played a role in their offending behaviour. Daryl grew up in an abusive environment and explained, "It's your upbringing; if you're brought up in a nice, happy family you'd probably feel sorry [for your crime]. But if you're brought up with lots of drinking and violence, you're just going to think it's normal." Ron stated that not only does he have a reputation for being "a tough guy," which he has to try to maintain, but his father does also. "I've seen my dad fight lots. He's got a good name too, so he doesn't want to ruin his reputation by getting beat up." This led to detrimental parental expectations. Ron explained that when he gets in a fight and comes home bloody, his dad is only concerned about knowing that his son did not lose the fight.

Although the authorities did recognize early violent victimization as a variable in youth criminality, their explanations seldom went beyond pathologizing individual family life and almost never incorporated more far-reaching structural paradigms. In fact, official explanations of youth crime—grounded firmly in individual and family circumstance—offer only a myopic appreciation of the roles played by institutional racism, economic and social inequality and cultural difference. As Lilly et al. recognize, "[T]he revitalization of individualistic theory … [ignores any] consideration of how long-standing patterns of inequality in power and living conditions are implicated in these criminogenic 'deficiencies'" (1995:219–20).

The authorities' failure to recognize the influence and interconnection of structural factors is illustrated in their reference to substance abuse as an individual problem rather than a problem in one's upbringing. As one psychologist specified, "Someone who has the propensity to act in assaultive ways is more likely to do so when inhibitions are diminished." The psychiatrist stated:

I have assessed twenty-five murderers so far and I cannot recall one case where the youth had not been drinking. I believe that they would not have killed if substance abuse was not involved.... Most kids are just ignorant, naive and drunk, and someone says something to them and there you go.

The message is that youths respond violently when substance abuse removes inhibitions and reveals true character; beyond that, there is no appreciation of the childhood origins of such behaviour nor any acknowledgement that youths might be seen as victims rather than perpetrators. Schissel explains:

As with personality problems, parental problems and childhood abuse produce inordinately high levels of substance abuse, self-injurious behaviour, social isolation, poor physical and mental health, low incomes and involvement in prostitution. These consistent results suggest irrefutably that statutory youth are inordinately victimized and that their victimization leads to dangerous and detrimental behaviour and situations. (Schissel 1997:102)

Structural factors that were often misunderstood by authorities but of singular significance in the self-explanations of youths were the needs both for respect and for the adrenaline "rush" of being violent. When I asked Mark why he committed assault, he responded:

I just don't want to be screwed around. I guess it's an anger thing too; when someone tries to rip me off of money or drugs, calls my mom a name or beats up my little brother, I just freak.

Maintaining one's reputation and ties with friends is important enough to warrant violent behaviour. A connection to a peer group, although not necessarily a formal gang, has long been recognized as an integral part of youth culture, particularly on the streets. To the extent that self-respect was factored into official explanations of youth violence, it was usually individualized and re-interpreted by authorities as a sign of bad character and not as an outcome of social and economic inequality. Discussing the changes in youth crime, the constable detective suggested, "There's a big chip on the shoulder now; both Mom and Dad are working, there's less supervision of the kids, and more influence and pressure for young people to grow up so quickly." Similarly, a probation officer claimed, "They're so much more confrontational." What is absent from these explanations is the reality that, in a world where respect is increasingly equated with money, designer clothes and other symbols of material wealth, youths who do not have the means to consume in a consumerist society may face a crisis of self. In their attempt to gain a sense of self some youths find other means—destructive and often violent means—to assert their value, pride, strength and self-respect. Thus, the motivation for crime rooted in poverty, substance abuse, family victimization and unequal access to opportunities must be used to contextualize rather than individualize youths' quest for self-respect.

The structuralist dimension is also vital to an appreciation of the personal benefits of violence, particularly the adrenaline "rush." Artz (1998:188) emphasizes that we must understand what violence does for disadvantaged youth, and she cites Katz (1988) in her explanation of the "sensual dimensions" of violent behaviour. In Artz's study the participants commented on the rush and the excitement of "discharging their anger against the victim who had, after all, caused that anger in the first place" (1998:188). The majority of assaultive youths in my study indicated that, initially at least, violence was a release and a rush. Katie stated: "At first it's like, oh my God, I can't believe I'm doing this. And then it was like something inside that just got big, and I don't know if it was having that power over [the victim]." Artz (1998:189) asserts that the youths' common reference to their victims as "sluts" or "assholes" "suggests a unilateral construction of one's opponents as detestable and worthy only of contempt.… [T]his is a graphic indictment of a life-world in which violence and abuse are part of the fabric of everyday life." For example, Ron explained that fighting "gets your anger out and it's a rush. You get rid of anger when you inflict pain on someone else; I feel better after I just punch someone out if he deserved it." He also indicated that punching a wall isn't satisfying because "you can't inflict pain on the wall."

It must be noted that the front-line workers interviewed, such as probation officers, had more contact with youths and thus were more in tune with youth reality and more cognizant of structural barriers. Often, as Kelly (1992:35) notes, lower level professionals pay lip service to the processes that identify and support their expertise, even though their experience with youths signals an ambivalence toward the treatment rationale. In a discussion of the differences between violent and non-violent youths, the professionals relied on individualized explanation. One of the psychologists, for instance, stated that "the distinction lies in the youth's own perception of what's appropriate. Many don't cross the line of physical aggression." Similarly, the psychiatrist claimed that "aggressive kids express more outwards, [and are] macho, but sexual offenders are more socially inadequate, quiet, shy and timid." In comparison, the front-line workers recognized the connection between structural factors and the commission of crime. One of the probation officers commented that early victimization often leads to violence and a loss of opportunity:

> Types that don't have a violent background that get involved is more random. Violent behaviour shows up at nearly every stage: they don't do well in school, [and there are] repeated acts of violence when they get older which becomes more serious.

The front-line workers were also more sensitive in their approach to violent youths. A different probation officer gave the example of a Vietnamese youth who saw his brother killed, his mother raped and his father disappear in the course of a year:

> We can't inflict punishment on this kid; it will make him worse. Fifty to sixty percent of the youth at the specialized unit are Vietnamese, and this is something that has blipped [in the stats]. Aboriginals are also grossly over-represented, which brings a whole new set of issues in terms of family dysfunction, sexual and physical abuse and race.

Despite the sensitivities of front-line staff, most authorities did not clearly recognize, or were ambivalent about, the role of structural factors in youth violence. In addition, structural barriers, such as poverty, lack of access to education and jobs, family abuse, low social status and racism were not identified by the authorities as being interconnected. The youths, however, did acknowledge the role of such barriers in the commission of crime. Clearly, the youths' daily experience of living on the margins of society is seldom appreciated within professional discourse.

Perhaps the most important goal of this study is to relay how the youths and the authorities perceive "the violent youth." It is obvious that the use of the medical model and the ways in which youths are classified and their experience typified in professional discourse have led to an inaccurate portrait of the violent youth. Stereotypes, by definition, are distortions of reality that often serve other social purposes in the adult world. They represent an additional layer of illusion, masking and detracting from the reality of life experienced by youths. These professional stereotypes of youths become entrenched in society through continual reaffirmation in the media.

The Violent Girl and Media Representation

Although the discourse on youth crime has always focused on the increase in the number and severity of violent acts, the newly perceived threat of the violent girl has sparked particular curiosity and panic. Girls committing assault and murder and the rise of girl gangs have commanded public attention. Female toughness and aggression are often perceived as a betrayal of the sex, and authorities are scrambling to explain the change in disposition. Female violence is particularly topical throughout the media. During the interviews, I was made aware of a recent documentary produced by the CBC, *Nasty Girls*, which focuses on the experience of some of the female respondents in this study. The girls reacted negatively to how they were portrayed, and their interpretation signifies a real disjuncture in the understanding of young female violence. The commentary in the film featured "expert testimony," which offers powerful interpretations of how to comprehend the violent girl (Schissel 1997).

Nasty Girls

To better understand the reaction of my female respondents I obtained a copy of the CBC documentary *Nasty Girls*, which was broadcast on March 5, 1997. Obviously the production was shaped by "expert" knowledge on violent girls. It begins with old black and white film footage of two little girls playing with dolls. The voice-over explains that "some things are at the heart of every little girl." The next scene, a little girl ironing with her mom, is accompanied by the comment: "Mother's little helper is learning to become a home-maker." The screen goes black and a female voice authoritatively asserts that "things have changed in the 1990s." The theme song, "Gangster Paradise," begins to play as pictures of provocative young women on magazine covers flash across the screen. The accompanying caption reads: "Naughty but nice." This is followed by scenes of police car lights, girls running around dark street corners and the voice of one female offender listing the crimes she has committed. Newspaper headlines proclaiming "Girls' violence reported on rise" and "Girls in gangs" flash over re-occurring scenes of a fight and female offenders behind bars. The reporter begins by pointing out the arrival of a new age: "In the late 1990s almost everything your mother taught you about polite society has disappeared from popular culture and nowhere is this more apparent than in what is happening to our teenage girls." Welcome to the age of the "nasty girls."

This obvious romanticism with the past and dichotomy between former good girls and the present "nasty girls" are constant themes throughout the film. At a point when the camera is touring the girls' cells, the reporter states, "And then there are the mementoes that remind you that the violent teenager was, not too many years ago, somebody's little girl … but the crimes committed by somebody's little girl would shock you." The camera zooms into one of the girls' cells and onto a calendar depicting angels. The reporter reiterates that the owner of the calendar "is anything but an angel…. Her story, according to experts, is a classical case study in the making of a violent girl."

The documentary distinguishes not only between the past and present, but also between "ordinary" and violent girls, pathologizing those who were arrested for committing violent acts. Before eliciting comments on how high school girls perceive girl violence, the interviewer invites us to "Listen to the voices, not of young offenders, but of ordinary girls in a Vancouver high school." In one segment introduced by text that reads, "Once the repository of sugar and spice and everything nice…" we see black-and-white footage of three young women on a beach. Then the text "Today young women celebrate materialism, aggressive sexuality and nasty behaviours" is illustrated by the image of an attractive black woman with a jewel between her teeth, who eventually puts her hand over the face of a man trying to get her attention. As Schissel comments, "The 'sugar and spice' understanding of femaleness is often the standard upon which young female offenders are judged and, in effect, the images of 'bad girls' are presented as … sinister products of the feminist movement" (1997:107). The film implies that young girls' aggressive, wild and dominating behaviour is an attempt to emulate boys, which, "experts" explain, results in boys and girls performing comparable acts of violence. This is otherwise known as "horizontal violence." As Andrea stated during her interview, "Girls my age don't put up with shit any more." Overall, the film suggests that, in comparison to the "sugar" of the past, there is something very different about today's girls, particularly those who engage in violence.

Nasty Girls essentially mirrors official discourse on the nature of youth violence, albeit in staged format. Sibylle Artz, director of the School of Child and Youth Care at the University of Victoria, is the "expert" in the film. Coming from a psychology background, Artz is susceptible to the professional tendency to individualize youth crime by judging youth as incapable of taking responsibility. She also contributes to moral panic over the issue by highlighting cases that fit the stereotypes found in official understanding. One girl, incarcerated in Victoria for her involvement in the murder of the pimp, speaks in the film about her life of family violence. She also describes the murder scene, briefly mentioning that the girls were drinking as a prelude to beating and drowning the pimp. The youth ended her description of the murder with the statement: "It just happened." But for Artz, such an explanation is inadequate. As she explains to the audience, "It didn't just happen, they threw him in the culvert. The way it's described is as if that's an object that got carried away by some force bigger than everyone, and the whole question of responsibility is completely absent there." For most proponents of the professional discourse, there is an enduring need to individualize responsibility, to blame youths for their actions and to ignore structural factors that may mediate or contextualize youth violence. Moreover, as if to confirm all the worst stereotypes about violent youth, the documentary's reporter observes that "the staff [in Willingdon] echo what those on the outside say: the girls are getting harder, the crimes nastier and the question of how to de-program the violent girl is becoming more urgent."

Near the end of the film, the camera focuses on the girls working at computers with the ironic commentary, "So in the safety and predictability of the institution, the violent girls work on basic life skills ... as they prepare to go back out into a world that will not welcome them." The reporter then cites Artz as saying, "These wounded children who have become nasty skaters, rappers and fashion freaks are like mirrors: reflecting all that is wrong in consumer culture." The film ends with the text of Artz's words superimposed on more images of the violent girl:

> [W]e've lost a sense of a spirited self, we've lost a sense of community, our kids at the margins are giving us the loudest and clearest messages about it: give us back a way to belong, a way to have value for ourselves, not to see ourselves as objects, love us, stay connected with us, hear us.

Reaction from the Nasty Girls: Youths' Reality Ignored

The media was a real source of contention with the girls in YDC, particularly those who had participated in *Nasty Girls*. Katie explained:

> The reporters asked about our violent crimes and then if we felt bad, but they didn't show that part; they only showed the part where we were talking about the violence and they played "Gangster Paradise" as the theme song.

According to Andrea:

> They made us look so bad. They made me look like some psycho-chick. They showed me fidgeting, which I do when I'm nervous. You know the beginning where they show girls kicking the shit out of the other girl ... the voice-over is me. I didn't even know they were taping that. They asked what I did and I told them that I am sorry and I want the victim to know, but they didn't put that in of course.

83

Andrea continued to explain that much of the presentation was staged. "I look like some sort of gangster; they said when you walk by [the camera] make sure you touch your hand on the fence." The producers were obviously attempting to make the girls appear mischievous and restless as if to validate their need for incarceration and perhaps to warn viewers of the potential danger once these "trapped animals" are released.

It is precisely this type of "news" coverage that supports Acland's (1995) interpretation that the concept of "Other" is integral to the creation of "youth in crisis." The youths' explanation that they felt bad or that they had intentions of being productive working citizens made them too ordinary and therefore was not of interest to the media authorities involved in producing the film. A focus on the young girls' violent behaviour enforces the conceptual boundaries of "youth" and "child" from which violent girls are excluded. The identification of difference is essential to the ruling relations and to constructing and maintaining social order. The increased attention to female youth violence in movies, newspapers and media in general has produced what Acland calls "the politics of spectacle" (1995:14). The focus is no longer on the facts of the initial crime; it is on the notion that violence among young girls is out of control.

As Acland (1995) further argues, the voice of youth is not included in the discourse on youth violence because their perspective may dismantle the constructs that nourish societal panic. In addition, it would be uneconomical to develop adequate solutions; normalcy does not sell. Two of the girls whom I interviewed refused to take part in the *Nasty Girls* documentary because, as Tara indicated, "I didn't want to have anything to do with it.… They really conned everyone. It was like look down your noses at these kids, look what you're breeding; people don't want to see that you felt bad." A large part of the film focused on the details of the three girls who had murdered their pimp, but the one whom I interviewed, Jane, refused to be part of it: "I'm not going to go on national T.V. and broadcast so they can make money." Jane's comment suggests how some youths are cognizant of Acland's claim that the concept of "youth in crisis" generates an entire industry sustained by sensational media. Although Jane agreed that violence among girls is increasing, in reference to the film she said: "I think the media looked at the wrong thing; they looked at what [the girls] do but not why. They don't care; they just want to make money." Moreover, she astutely pointed out that the media consistently fail to focus on how degrading and violent prostitution is for the girls involved.

Decontextualized Rates of Female Violence

Media often decontextualizes the acts of crime for public consumption. When youth crime is presented in a "social, economic and political vacuum, it appears as if nothing else is occurring in society except kids doing bad things" (Schissel 1997:73). Most of the establishment authorities agreed that there were ever-increasing numbers of girls involved in violent crimes. One of the psychiatric social workers asserted, "I've been working with kids since the late '60s and I've seen more females involved in violent acts, more involved in gangs; it may be a wannabe type of situation." One of the probation officers stated that girls become involved in violence because of "trivial stuff, such as someone making a bad comment." She also stated that the number of girls involved in violent crime has increased but "not necessarily to the level of violence of the boys."

The youths I talked with provided a context for any increase in female violence. For example, Katie indicated: "People see that violence is coming out in girls more, and I think that's right; but I think that's just because a lot of violence against girls is increasing too in general." Jane explained that judgements about violent girls and rates of violence do not include a recognition of the situation: "Circumstances should be a big thing, but I just don't think the judge looks past the exhibits." Thus, there should be a recognition of circumstances in the youth world relative to their own existence and experience, as opposed to circumstances important to the criminal justice system situated in the adult world.

Media and the Recycling of Stereotypes

The authorities and the youths had somewhat different perceptions of the effects of the media in furthering youth criminality. One psychologist commented, "The youth we see have very strange ideas about cause and effect." He referred to how violence is glorified in movies and how youths think they can walk away. He gave the example of a youth who claimed he knocked a woman out so he could steal her money, but the reality was that he beat her to death with a barbell. The pathologist in the case stated that he had never seen such damage, indicating that her skull was completely caved in. Apparently, the youth assumed the victim would regain consciousness. Similarly, the psychiatrist said that in general the youths "copy someone":

> They flash the knife like Chuck Norris, use a gun in a certain way, kick or punch a guy in the head like they've seen in the movies. The movie may not bring them to that situation, but when they are doing the offence they emulate certain actions.

However, when I questioned the youths, several disagree with the establishment authorities about the extent to which movies contributed to violence. Tara commented:

> I think it can contribute [to violence] but you have to be a really moldable kid; there are things in movies that kids imitate but I think it has to hit a sick kid to make them. I think everyone's trying to shift the blame on something instead of looking in families.

Some of the establishment authorities also commented that Canadian youths imitate American trends portrayed in the media. One psychiatric social worker stated:

> It's unbelievable how they try to emulate a culture they've never been a part of; two or three kids have said they wish they were Black because that's what they feel like: no future. Even though they've never been south of the border or in that culture, they witness it through T.V. and movies so it's real.

A probation officer indicated that youth copy other trends in the United States, such as car-jacking or "curbing," whereby the victim's head is put on a curb and stomped. According to one psychiatric social worker some kids were into "ritual stuff": "They do tend to like more violence; their anger connects with the music they listen to." However, a youth observed:

> It's not so much the gangsta rap, it's the way people are interpretating it.... A lot of it talks about stopping Black-on-Black crime and stopping this bullshit. Violence would already be in the person; it may just help to provoke it.

Although the youths agreed that violent movies do desensitize, several remarked that there is a certain amount of violence in the adult world too. This illustrates one element of the disjuncture between the perceptions of youth and establishment authority; the latter refers to a *youth* culture based on crime without also acknowledging violence as part of the adult world. Katie commented that "violence is just so acceptable," citing an episode of the television cartoon *The Simpsons*. Tara stated that violence in society "is a big problem that is affecting every age group. People aren't doing anything any more.... They're getting used to it, [and] I think people are scared to try [to solve the problem]." One of the psychiatric social workers agreed: "Violence is at the heart of society.

Movies and music are merely a reflection of what's going on in society; they don't kill people ... they reduce the ability to empathize." Regarding violent music another authority stated:

> I think it's obvious [that] if you create a youth culture which at the base is the commission of crime, you're giving the message to young people that that's an acceptable way of behaving; the cause and effect is so obvious.

Thus, there was some agreement between the two groups on the effects of media misrepresentation. Katie stated: "I think [youth violence] is just more public because if half the people in the world didn't pick up the paper they wouldn't know there was violence. They don't see it in everyday lives; media just blows it up too much." One probation officer concurred. "I'm not down-playing that it's not a problem, but it's not growing like the media would like to suggest." "I don't think media covers courts very well any more," a judge commented. "Media happens to be at one particular case, and that becomes the big story. So media isn't sensationalizing per se, but I don't think it's very representative.... It does not follow through on stories." A youth convicted of murder claimed that media "don't even say anything about the good stuff, they just focus on the bad stuff." As Acland (1995:46) argues, media produce metaphors and connotations by associating an event with other familiar narratives, stories and events that already make sense to us: "Events do not speak their newsworthiness; rather, the culturally defined category stands as an informal set of criteria informing what is to enter a position of public and popular scrutiny."

Obviously the credibility of most "news" stories is based on expert testimony, which sifts fact from fiction and maintains an air of journalistic objectivity. The specialized knowledge and language of these experts are especially convincing. It is evident that, through media, the authorities have created what Schissel (1997) outlines as specific portraits of crime which filter out to the public and become accepted as reality. The first portrait is "the creation of a world of insiders and outsiders, and acceptability and unacceptability, in order to facilitate public demand and consumption" (Schissel 1997:17). This is illustrated in images of the good or "ordinary" youth and the bad or "violent" youth with a focus on the sensational as if it is a common occurrence. The second portrait is "the connecting of images of deviance and crime with social characteristics" (Schissel 1997:17) It was once believed that rock-and-roll was contributing to youth deviance; and, although the "causes" have changed, they still reflect elements that somehow threaten social order and the position of the powerful. According to Schissel (1997), the reality of youths clustering in groups and appearing idle in malls and street corners reflects how industry has "rationalized" production by reducing employment, lowering wages and offering few benefits, but the image presented is that youth are loitering with the intent to commit crime. The third portrait is the "decontextualization of crime in anecdotal evidence that is presented as omnipresent, noncomplex truth" (Schissel 1997:17), which is illustrated in the authorities' insistence that violence mainly stems from the personalities of the youths.

Media portrayals of violent youths are recognized as a contributing factor in popular perception. More disconcerting, however, is the effect media constructs seem to have on expert knowledge. *A Clockwork Orange* is a classic violent youth film that has provided a framework for how some authorities perceive youth and think about violence. According to Katie:

> The description of the police and judges was to compare the crime to *Clockwork Orange*. I didn't agree with comparing it to terror and mental problems and I didn't agree with the [assumption] that this fight started for no reason, because in the movie the fights and everything were just senseless.

Katie thought that such comparisons were made because

> the judge had to have an effect in the courtroom because the girl's parents were there for the whole trial. I think the judge must have been beaten up as a kid or something because my lawyers, even the Crown counsel said the judge was out of control; he just treated my case with a vengeance I guess.

The authorities not only are buying into their own stereotypes about youth violence; they are also equating these stereotypes with violent images in movies and the media.

Conclusion

Clearly portraits of crime painted by the media are reaffirmed by "expert" opinion, which often speaks more to the privileged position of the experts than to the lived reality of youths. Much of the problem with media misrepresentation stems from the disjuncture between youths' and establishment authorities' underlying understandings of youth violence.

> This contemporary medical/psychological discourse of good-
> ness and badness sets youth crime in a context of orthodox
> criminology: individuals gone wrong, either inherently or cul-
> turally. The underlying ideological position is that society is
> structured correctly and that individuals who offend are indi-
> vidually or socially pathological and identifiable. (Schissel
> 1997:105)

The authorities' views on violent youths are complicated, however;
and, in certain instances, they are negated or questioned by youths
themselves. Thus, the credibility of "expert" testimony is the result of
relations of ruling and positions of power. In the end, the respondents'
perception of the rate of and contributing factors to youth violence
generally, and female violence specifically, reaffirms the inconclusion
surrounding the parameters of youth violence outlined in Chapter One.
There is a need to abandon the search for the positivist notion of
"causality" and to recognize that antecedents are a reflection of time, of
place and of those who are in charge of defining reality.

Notes

1. Dr. Robert Hare developed the Psychopathy Checklist, which he describes as
    a "highly reliable diagnostic tool that any clinician or researcher [can] use
    and that yield[s] a richly detailed profile of the personality disorder called
    psychopathy" (1993:32). In his book *Without Conscience: The Disturbing World
    of the Psychopaths Among Us* (1993), Hare outlines the key symptoms of
    psychopathy, which are divided into two groups. The first group, "emo-
    tional/interpersonal" includes traits such as: glib and superficial, egocentric
    and grandiose, lack of remorse or guilt, lack of empathy, deceitful and
    manipulative and shallow emotions. Traits of the second group, "social
    deviance" include: impulsive, poor behaviour controls, need for excitement,
    lack of responsibility, early behaviour problems and adult antisocial behav-
    iour. Before describing the symptoms in detail, Hare provides a cautionary
    note: "Do not use these symptoms to diagnose yourself or others. A diagnosis
    requires explicit training and access to the formal scoring manual" (1993:34).

Chapter Four

The Youth Justice System and Inherent Contradictions in Perception

The disjuncture between the perceptions of youths and establishment authorities in comprehending and depicting violence, as outlined in Chapter Three, is relevant when examining how justice works as a "system" and what should and can be done about youth violence. The youth justice system is a multi-layered, hierarchical structure premised on the application of professional expertise to apprehending, sentencing and punishing young offenders. As such, it is an expression of both an institutional culture and a doctrine that are often resistant to ways of knowing from other sources. Among other things, this resistance negates the voices of those whom the system is meant to benefit. At the same time, justice takes place in a professionalized framework that is laced with apparent inconsistencies and seemingly mired in inertia where reform of the most violent youth is concerned.

The first section of this chapter details the youths' experience through each stage of the justice process, focusing on the irony of the youth rehabilitation process. Evidence clearly suggests that youths resist official discourse and yet appropriate it as part of their own sense-making. The data also demonstrate a contradiction between the efforts to rehabilitate violent youths and the violent context in which that rehabilitation takes place. The interview material also underscores the fact that, given the resistance of authorities to meaningful change, youth detention centres offer little hope for immediate reform, particularly in the case of violent youths.

The second section of this chapter addresses conflicting notions about the prospects of violent youths. Most young people entertain both utopian and realistic ideas of who they are and what they hope to become. But often the goals articulated by incarcerated youths are at odds with the means of attainment provided by justice authorities. The root of the inconsistency is the justice system's overwhelming tendency, in intellectualizing and designing programs for youths, to stress personality disorders and psychological solutions. As a result, there is limited appreciation of structural factors, such as poverty and a lack of opportunities, both as causes of youth crime and as valuable indicators of where meaningful reform must begin.

The System

The youth justice system is an adult enforcement/treatment mechanism designed to ensure conformity to status quo definitions of "normal" behaviour. It is meant to promote social stability and is based on long-standing relations of imposed authority. The system's entrenched nature is reflected in the conservative attitude of authorities and in the enduring reliance on incarceration as the main means of dealing with violent youths. Young offenders relate to the system as non-adult clients and objects of authority. They are both resistant to and enmeshed in the relations of ruling.

Youths' Experience with Authorities

The youths' perspective on the justice system can be constructed from their experience with the police and courts. Explicit in their descriptions is a dissonance between the perceptions and actions of authorities on the one hand and the self-articulated experiences of youths on the other. Police, lawyers and judges are an integral part of the ruling apparatus, and their perceptions of and reaction to youth violence are conditioned, if not governed, by the dogma of "enlightened" professional knowledge. Consequently, there arises the central issue of the incongruence between how professionals and how offenders themselves believe violent youth should be treated.

Schissel (1997) explains that, in responding to public and political demands and choosing what to make public, police unknowingly produce images of criminality. Because much of their mandate is based on crime prevention, it is not surprising that they often target those stereotyped as a threat. As Ron indicated:

> the police made it look like I was the bad guy, [even though] they weren't there to see what happened. They said I was still threatening him, but I was in the hospital the night it happened. I was out cold pretty much all night so I don't think that's a fair description.

In addition, because the police present crime accounts to public officials, they contribute to moral panic.

The police, as front-line workers, have vast credibility in the eyes of the public. Unfortunately, when they panic, their actions echo quickly, and their consequences and continual lack of reflexivity and self-analysis is potentially harmful for targets of public panics. (Schissel 1997:27)

This is illustrated in some of the youths' experiences with the police. Ron stated that the police broke his teeth, an action he couldn't understand because, he was "too drunk to resist": "I couldn't even walk. After the fight I was pretty disoriented, and they tried to say after the fight that I got out of the [police] car and swung at them." Garth experienced a similar situation:

I was being chased [by police], then I gave up and they beat me up. I had a broken nose, two black eyes, my ears were purple, two big cuts on my nose, broken ribs. When they brought me in, the jail said we can't accept him, he has to go to the hospital first. The police said I was reaching for a knife, that's why they had to re-strain me and use force, and they said that I fell down and hit my head getting into the paddywagon. They said all that just so they don't get in trouble. They don't like me because I've been in trouble with the police since I was eight years old, so they just did it.

The youth charged the police, and an internal investigation was apparently conducted.

Corrado et al. (1992:216) also detail the changing roles of court officials in their assessment of the impact of the Young Offenders Act. "The greatest enhancements of judges' roles have ... occurred with respect to their authority to impose custodial dispositions and to exercise direct control over the administration of these dispositions." In making a fully informed decision, judges also have the authority to order medical and psychological reports, an obvious reflection of their dependence on the medical model.

Despite the availability of massive reports on each offender, the youths' individual needs are not addressed. As Kelly argues, "processes of decision making which require the decision maker to take into account a large number of variables can in themselves generate arbitrariness. In such a situation, individuals display a tendency to focus upon the most simple and obvious variables" (1992:103). The most obvious variables in the case of youths are their age and their commission of a violent crime. The stereotypical underpinnings of violent youths obviously produce a certain reaction from some judges. For example, Tara stated, "The judge was really rude.... When he was sentencing us he was going on that we had no honesty and no credibility on the stand ... just stuff that he really didn't have to [say]." In addition, Ron said, "The judge blowed it way out of proportion. He made it look like I went there to fight, [but] we went there to have a good time. I never provoked it, but I was still found guilty."

It can be argued that judges share society's disdain for violent youths and contribute, through their sentencing, to the creation of a moral panic concerning youth violence. One of the judges with whom I spoke felt that the number of robberies occurring at Skytrain Stations was a real problem: "They almost always involve weapons (guns or knives). [The youths] are stealing bank cards and PIN numbers. They're usually done in groups, and there's always threats of violence if you tell." In dealing with the problem the judge explained that those appearing before him for sentencing are "all going to jail. The community is absolutely alarmed for good reason." The judge also indicated that the court needs more press coverage of how these crimes are punished.

Similarly, an analysis of the contradiction in the role of defence counsel reveals a stereotypical view of violent youth and the inherent disjuncture in perceptions. In their article, "Advocate or Guardian: The Role of Defence Counsel in Youth Justice," Milne et al. (1992) explain that establishing the youths' right to counsel under the Young Offenders Act was necessary to ensure that the interests of the child are represented.

> [C]ontradictions emerge [however] because the Declaration of Principles, s. 3 of the YOA, emphasizes supervision, discipline and control while simultaneously recognizing the special needs of young persons requiring guidance and assistance.... The rationale underlying the guardian role for defence counsel is that juveniles are perceived to have a lack of or limited capacity to identify and to effectively communicate their own best interests. (Milne et al. 1992:315, 317–18)

Although several youths understood the role of the various establishment authorities, they disagreed with their motives and recommendations. In Mark's case, the lawyer had told the judge that Mark felt bad about the assault, but the judge wanted to hear it from Mark himself. Mark explained, "It took me a few minutes and I thought, 'I'm not going to lie,' so I said, 'I don't feel bad at all.'"

Indeed, some youths were irritated by these "legal games" and expressed an ironic defiance of adult dishonesty. Katie commented, "[The lawyers] are so different in the little room than in the court room. They said, 'Cry for me if you can,' [but] I didn't." Her sister, Tara, was told by her lawyer to say that she didn't hit the victim because she had a good

Giving Youth A Voice

chance of being found not guilty: "But despite what everyone told me to do, I pleaded guilty." Garth claimed:

> If I did it, I always plead guilty. There's no point going to trial if I did it. If you get caught lying you get more time so you might as well admit to it and do your sentence and get it over with.

Critics of the advocacy role of defence counsel suggest "that the apparent failure of the treatment philosophy of the court and the informality of procedure does not warrant the use of legal technicalities to get their client 'off', if help or treatment is needed" (Milne et al. 1992:319). Therefore, although the youths' criticism stems from valuing honesty in its own right, adult critics think the child should not be encouraged to deceive the judge because they "perceive delinquency as an illness requiring treatment in order that the person may return to a state of normalcy" (Milne et al. 1992:319).

The Violent Institution: An Unrealistic Site for Programming

The disjuncture in how the authorities perceive violent youths and how the youths perceive themselves, as detailed in Chapter Three, is compounded by the treatment of youths once they are sentenced to custody. To better understand the difficulties with programming, it is necessary to provide context to the institution and detail some daily activity.

There is no segregation between violent and non-violent offenders in Willingdon, except for males who have committed murder, who are housed in a separate unit at night. It is, however, well known which youths are part of that unit because, as Todd stated, "A lot of kids in here are scared of us. They think if they piss us off we'll hurt them."

All girls, regardless of their crime, are in one unit. Katie commented:

> I like having so few girls in here because we're in a unit that fits eleven girls comfortably. When we get counts as high as twenty-five it's hell. [The staff] put us in gym programs with just the girls, and ten of them are coming down from using some kind of drug like heroin or coke, so they don't want to participate. They shouldn't be in jail; they should be in a rehab program.

The majority of the youths' waking hours are spent at school. Garth explained, "It doesn't take long to finish here. We got computers, and you take homework back to your unit. All my school since grade seven has been done in jail." As an extension of the school at Willingdon, there is the Genesis Program, which is taught by those educated and experienced in dealing with violent youth. The program takes place at the probation

94

office, so there is also access to one-to-one workers and the job placement counsellor.

One probation officer explained that the Youth Specialized Supervision Unit employs an intensive supervision model, making it a program in itself. Officers in this unit have half the caseload of a regular probation officer, "with the goal of providing more intensive monitoring and program referral." He also explained that contact with the youths in every aspect of their lives, including school and family, is more frequent.

Although there is, in fact, no specific programming to curb violent behaviour, anger management both inside and outside the institution is often prescribed. It is the focus of a program called the *Unloading Zone*, which is conducted by a psychologist who is also an anger management specialist trained in the corrections field. The anger management programs target teenagers, and some are culture-specific. The Youth Court Services workers do not treat female sex offenders nor do they have specific anger management for females because, as was indicated by one psychologist, "We don't ever get enough to do a group of anything because their numbers are low."

A psychiatric social worker explained that anger management is based on a "cognitive behaviour model in which the modules include looking at the problem cycle; understanding needs, are they met; specific control techniques; empathy; covert sensitization on a one-to-one basis; planning; social skills; communications skills; and sex ed." According to *Abnormal Psychology*:

> [The cognitive paradigm] focuses on how people structure their experiences, how they make sense of them, transforming environmental stimuli into information that is useable ... cognitively oriented behaviour therapists attempt to change the thinking process of their patients in order to influence their emotions and behaviour. (Davison and Neale 1994:50-51)

Another psychiatric social worker indicated that "all the work we do is cognitive-based training—trying to get them to understand why, what's got them there and what might get them there again." There are various one-to-one counselling options for violent and sexual offenders; for instance, the one-to-one adult workers spend a lot of time with the youths and act as mentors. The youths also have access to counselling from the authorities at Youth Court Services and one-to-one discussions with correctional staff, such as the officer in charge of programming (OCP). As the OCP explained, "I hear too many times the kids say, 'Well, [the victims are] covered by insurance, they'll get ... back [the money from the stolen merchandise].' I spend a lot of one-to-one time with the kids, and I'm always trying to point out to them how it feels." She used the example of a youth who "went off the deep end" because his shampoo and deodorant were stolen. The OCP tried to use the opportunity to point out how it feels to be victimized: "You have to take every opportunity you can to stop them and point it out. They really respond to this, [but] I don't think we do enough of that." The OCP explained that she had tried repeatedly to bring in "victim groups" to discuss the consequences of youths' violence. There was little response, however, due to the belief that the youths could cause more damage by being non-responsive.

Other programs focus on self-esteem and related issues. An outline of the program *On Solid Ground* includes discussion on the following three topics. "Lookin' at Life" ... examines the process of incremental change; how we gradually get used to things which causes us to have an unclear picture of reality and limits our awareness." "Caught in a Mind Trap" probes the "downward thinking spiral of worthlessness, hostility and helplessness." "Barrier to Change" investigates "how preconditioned beliefs and the 'I can't do that trap' are barriers to change." Other topics focus on attitude, self-image and building a strong sense of self. The program was described by Daryl, one of the incarcerated youths, as concentrating "on a lot of self-talk [and] convincing yourself that you don't have to do this [violence]."

The director of YCS described the institution:

> Willingdon houses the worst of the worst kids with re-offending rates as high as 90 percent. The youth justice system works in the sense that it streamlines kids. Those who are not chronic are not ending up in Willingdon; the worst are. We're dealing with staffing restrictions, money, space problems and an ethic of vulnerability [in the sense that] the kids don't want to disclose, and then face kids back in the units out of group. Kids are self-interested. We need to appeal to that fact, appeal to their business sense. We need to teach them that the costs of crime are high for them personally, and how to set goals for the future. We are therefore not trying to make them into warm, fuzzy individuals.

The institution's official purpose is to provide a secure place where offenders learn to repattern their violent behaviour. However, an obvious problem—highlighted by the voice of youths—is the violent context in which the programs, in particular anger management, take place. Almost all of the respondents described Willingdon as a "violent place" that breeds further violence among the youths. Garth stated:

I'm not a violent person, but in here I'm violent because if people pull a pen on me and they want to fight, I get real mad and I think of ways to get them back. I've been stabbed three times already.

The authorities' ignorance of the importance youths place on respect is also problematic. Maintaining a "good" reputation inside prison was described by the youths as contributing to violence, but there was no official recognition of the fact. For example, Clint's only violent crimes occurred while he was in prison because, as he indicated:

> They all say I won't fight back so they take advantage of me. I had enough. It was wrong but I had to make a stand that I wasn't going to take shit from anybody else any more ... and I gained respect as a result. You need to establish yourself with your peers here. The staff can think the best of you but you live with these guys for the duration of your sentence.

Similarly, after his murder charge Dave claimed:

> I never wanted to hit a guy again; I was scared shitless. I had nightmares and stuff. [But once in prison] all these big guys started giving me a hard time because I wouldn't fight. I just couldn't take it any more so I started fighting back. I didn't want to but that's the only way I could stop from getting shots. It was wrong but I had to make a stand.

Ron explained that maintaining one's reputation can lead to murder: "No one wants to lose, and no one gives up."

The institution's reliance on the medical model and a focus on individual behaviour deny that the youths are incarcerated in a violent environment. It is ironic that youths are expected to participate in anger management to rethink the situation and the reaction and to learn more productive ways of using their emotions in a place where one must be violent to survive. It is not surprising, therefore, that the youths see no benefit in such programs. Jacqueline Barkley (1998:315) further problematizes the issue:

> The recent enthusiasm for anger management suggests that our children must have been born with a new gene for anger. Since even the most foolish proponent of medicalizing social behaviour has not yet discovered such a gene, we must ask why we are treating the real and extensive anger among our children and

youth as a psychological and personal problem rather than as a manifestation of profound social dysfunction? (Barkley 1998:315)

In addition, the techniques of anger management assume unrealistic situations, considering that the youths often confront physically violent people in the real world. For example, Katie stated:

> I've been ordered to go to so much anger management and they're all the same. All it does is make you aware of the technical terms, like different kinds of abuse. If someone is coming at you, ready to hit you, you don't say "Oh, I'll be the bigger man and walk away." It doesn't work.

Tara described it as "awful": "This guy just said, 'Crumple your anger up and put it in your back pocket and take a deep breath,' and I was like, 'That's just not going to work.' It was really patronizing."

In her discussion of the power of language to reconstruct images of coercion, Kelly (1992:128) explains that, "professionals [in the institution] have been socialised to see their actions as rehabilitative procedures, not as constraints." Although the voice of youth could dismantle these constructs and although establishment authority claimed to be interested in the youths' opinions, it did not seem likely that the concept of anger management would be abandoned. Although one of the psychologists recognized the limitation of any anger management program conducted in an institutional setting, he maintained that it "is helpful [for] recognizing the impact of experience, understanding attitudes and how they influence learning. But there needs to be more adequate time and continuity." I find difficulty in recognizing such a program as "helpful" when not one youth I spoke with agreed. Similarly, a psychiatric social worker stated that "a lot of the programs are not very effective and could be made better by the perspective of someone who has gone through the programs." This sincerity was put in doubt , however, when she explained that "they'll love the attention, you're talking to them and spending time with them," as if paying lip-service to their ideas rather than recognizing the youths as "knowers" of their own situation. When I asked Ron if he had ideas for other programs he said: "I've never thought about it; no one has ever come to me and asked if I would like to go to this program or how I felt about them."

Perhaps the biggest problem with any programming, which is recognized by both youths and establishment authorities, is that what is taught inside the institution does not correspond to the youths' daily experience on the outside. For example, Josh stated: "It's just that when I'm in here I seem to think a lot more about my family and what I'm doing, but when

I'm out there I start doing it again." The youths undergo what Smith (1987) describes as a "bifurcation of consciousness," a disjuncture between the consciousness organized with the relations of ruling in the institution and a consciousness connected to daily life. The OCP at Willingdon explained that if anger management, for example, is beneficial at some level, it is only while the youth is incarcerated:

> In here kids deal with their anger, they don't act out. So when I see this I think a lot of them do have ways of managing their behaviour. But the problem with any programming done inside this building is there is no opportunity for them to practise the skills they learn. They often go back to everything they ever came from, and there's no one to point out to them when to use the skills.

Although the incongruence between life inside and outside of prison is recognized by the OCP as an inherent problem with programming, other establishment authorities blame the youths for not understanding, which may be why little has been done to remedy the situation. Graham commented on being institutionalized: "I don't know, it doesn't seem to be worth it. I just keep coming in and out. [They need] something harder than this; this place is a joke." Josh stated, "I'm trying to be on the right track because I know that after this time I'll get an adult record; they'll raise me. But I've said that it's the last time like five times ago." In light of these comments one psychiatric social worker indicated, "Sometimes kids need wake-up calls but the longer they're in there, the worse off they are because it becomes a learning/survival situation. They do not understand that what works in jail does not work on the outside."

Hence, there is a disjuncture not only between the perception of authorities and youths but also between front-line workers and those authorities who have less communication with the offenders. Of all adult respondents in this study, the OCP has perhaps the most daily contact with the youths. It is not surprising, therefore, that she also recognizes the inconsistencies and problems with programming within the institution. Similarly, one of the probation officers described programs like cognitive skills training as "over-rated": "Within detention centres you're teaching [the youths] to be apathetic, but the subgroups within the centre become more powerful on a day-to-day basis—more important than an hour session." As Kelly correctly counters,

> [W]ithout the prestige associated with higher professionals and the unassailable power which elite knowledge groups such as psychiatrists have acquired, the lower level professionals … are

left to deal first hand with the all too obvious disparity between rhetorical and euphemistic imagery on the one hand, and the experience of the absence, or at least the inefficacy, of attempts to render welfare ideology workable in a penal environment on the other. (1992:109)

Thus, the voices of youths (and those authorities who appreciate their perspective) should be incorporated into correcting these failing programs instead of being ignored or their owners blamed.

Reliance on Incarceration

Obviously the "official" response of punishing serious criminals has been to send them to jail. The value of incarceration is yet another age-old topic of debate among professionals. In his book *Punishment and Modern Society: A Study in Social Theory*, Garland (1990:1) explains how, as a social policy,

> [punishment] is a continual disappointment, seeming always to fail in its ambitions and to be undercut by crises and contradictions of one sort or another. As a moral or political issue, it provokes intemperate emotions, deeply conflicting interests, and intractable disagreements.

Rarely does professional discourse deal with the fact that the intended result and supposed benefit of being incarcerated are not realized if the offenders themselves perceive the sentence as neither punishment nor treatment.

Most youths indicated that they did not feel as if they were being punished. "Oh no," Katie stated, "because I don't do drugs or smoke, I'm not missing anything. The sports are good, the school here is really good, and the staff aren't strict; it's just that you don't have the freedom to go out and stuff." Several youths commented that they did not feel punished because they are treated like children. "This place ain't even like jail, it's like kid's day-camp. You're treated like a child. You're not allowed to swear, can't smoke and we have early bed times." The youths who did feel punished were substance-dependent. "The worst goes on when you're in your room alone at night [and] you don't have drugs or alcohol," Tara commented.

These sentiments support Foucault's (1979) claim that prisons are no longer seen as places of "punishment" in the traditional sense. In Foucault's history of modern punishment, *Discipline and Punish: The Birth of the Prison* (1979), he chronicles the change in penal technology from the scaffold, in which public ceremonies of violence against the offender were to serve as a deterrent, to the penitentiary, in which discipline is made private and silent using methods of sanctioning called "normalization" (Garland 1990:145). The target of punishment is now the offender's "soul" as opposed to the "body."

> This method is essentially corrective rather than punitive in orientation, concerned to induce conformity rather than to exact retribution or expiation. It involves, first of all, a means of assessing the individual in relation to a desired standard of conduct: a means of knowing how the individual performs, watching his movements, assessing his behaviour, and measuring it against the rule. Surveillance arrangements and examination procedures provide this knowledge, allowing incidents of non-conformity or departures from set standards to be recognized and dealt with, at the same time "individualizing" the different subjects who fall under this gaze. (Garland 1990:145)

Foucault recognizes that the more that is known, the more controllable it becomes; consequently, the more the authorities know about the offender, the greater their control and power. I would argue, however, that what is professionally "known" about the youths is inaccurate because it does not take into account their perspective. As Tara stated, "I don't think I need to be here for anything of my own, but I think I need to be here for them to say that they've punished me."

Some of the authorities referred to incarceration as beneficial in the sense of changing deviant behaviour. One judge explained that prison can be a good "wake-up call" for some youths but that "prisons are most effective when it's right away and short." This echoes the 1980s, British policy of "short, sharp, shock" detention orders (Corrado et al. 1992:140), a practice that has been dismissed as non-beneficial (Lipsey 1992). Finckenauer (1982) also recognizes that getting tough with past or future offenders does not seem to scare them straight (cited in Lilly et al. 1995:221). Other youths, the judge indicated, "benefit because they are kept out of the community and the influence of alcohol and drugs. They hopefully learn to repattern their behaviour." The absurdity of trying to create normal functioning in an abnormal environment has been repeatedly emphasized (Kelly 1992). And as Mark suggests, it does not work: "You get more and more used to this place. You think about how you're going to stay out of jail but when I get out I think about being out so who cares."

The basic assumption underlying behavioural approaches to the modification of delinquent behaviour is that behaviour is responsive to environmental factors and may be modified by its consequences (Yule 1977 cited in Kelly 1992:129). In institutions this approach is applied with the belief that positive behaviour followed by pleasant consequences is likely to increase, whereas negative behaviour followed by unpleasant consequences will decrease. The frequent application of this technique in institutions such as Willingdon has been via token economy systems (Ayllan and Azuin 1968), in which an inmate has to "earn" all privileges through "good" behaviour. The youths are assigned points for participation, co-operation, relations, hygiene and authority; the points are calculated and translated into "allowed spending." There are other rewards for good behaviour, such as being allowed to wear "personals" (i.e., their own shoes). Point deductions and status change occur when there is an "incident" or when the youth misbehaves. For example, Andrea scored poorly on authority because she was "slow to complete chores." If youths display specific "abnormal" conduct, they are placed on "risk observation" during which time the staff logs their behaviour on the half-hour. This occurred, for example, when a noose was found hidden in Andrea's bed.

This approach reflects one aspect of Foucault's normalization process. "'The examination' is, for this system, a central method of control, allowing close observation, differentiation, assessment of standards, and the identification of any failure to conform" (Garland 1990:145). Because the professional objective is to correct rather than punish, sanctions involve measures which help bring conduct into line and ensure that the individuals are more self-controlled. However, research on the token economy system suggests that it may aid institutional management (Burchard and Harig 1976), "but such limited evidence as is available shows no long-term benefits with respect to reduced recidivism rates" (Kelly 1992:129).

That privilege systems are implemented to benefit the institution more than the youth is illustrative of Foucault's understanding of the "body" and "power":

> For Foucault, as for Nietzsche and more recent authors such as Deleuze and Guattari, the human body is the ultimate material which is seized and shaped by all political, economic and penal institutions. Systems of production, of domination, and of socialization fundamentally depend upon the successful subjugation of bodies. More specifically, they require that bodies be mastered and subjected to training so as to render them docile, obedient, and useful to a greater or lesser degree. Some institutions [such as the prison] ... aim to have their commands internalized, producing an individual who habitually does what is required without need of further external force. (Garland 1990:137)

Thus, according to Foucault, power refers to the various forms of domination and subordination and the uneven balance of forces that operate in social relations. "In this sense power operates 'through' individuals rather than 'against' them and helps constitute the individual who is at the same time its vehicle" (Garland 1990:138). In her study Kelly (1992:178) found that staff members attempt to manipulate child leaders so that they will come to accept staff authority and use their influence over other inmates to inspire conformity. This is evident among youths who have committed murder and are housed in Willingdon's Unit Four, which contains pool tables, a television, microwaves and a Nintendo set. When I asked Dave how he would respond to people who think that murderers do not deserve such things, he stated: "I agree it's pretty good, but we're the best behaved kids in this place. We know what we're doing, we've got our routines down, [and] there's no concerns because we're all friends. The staff love working in our unit because we've been in here a long time." It appears that when "befriending" becomes part of the power relationship, "subordination via coercion" is blurred with the implicit aim of encouraging inmates to internalize the norms of establishment authority (Kelly 1992:177).

In direct contrast to official ideals of a prison environment that is conducive to changing violent behaviours, almost all of the youths commented that being in Willingdon does not reduce violence. For example, one psychiatric social worker observed: "For some it's the most secure environment that they've had; it's relatively safe and they get to know and like the people." Similarly, the constable detective claimed, "A lot of them love being in there. They'll say to me, 'Oh I get to go back and see my friends.' It's a safe place to sleep; their home environment may be so brutal that Willingdon is better." Although I do not deny that several youths have experienced violent homes, life inside Willingdon does not appear to be much different. Katie confirmed this:

> Two of my friends [in the youth detention centre] jumped on this girl and beat her up for writing a statement against [one of the girls] on the wall, and there were two other fights in my unit last night. So it doesn't reduce violence at all; if anything, it brings it out more. There are fights all the time in here; but if you put 120 people together you've gotta expect fights.

Tara indicated that the institution breeds violence: "[The youths] are worse when they get out. They come in here for stealing a car and by the time they get out they know what guns to use for an armed robbery."

Obviously the goals of prison are not realized, which makes it inconceivable that the use of secure custody for youths is increasing

(Corrado et al. 1992:235). In her study, Kelly notes that "the rhetorical imagery of welfare and benevolence, and of professional expertise in achieving rhetorical aims was profoundly contradicted by the penal nature of the unit's architecture and the level of constraint, coercion and surveillance it imposed" (1992:207). The knowledge base of the professionals and their discretion appear arbitrary and irrelevant. But as Cohen (1985) points out:

> [T]he system is not destroyed by its inherent irrationality, since its rationale is quite clearly other than the stories it may tell about itself…. The secure unit itself is one point in the overall juvenile justice system where, because of the existence of very clear, stark contrasts between rhetoric and reality, the central ideological conflict of welfare and coercion emerge in a most obvious way. (cited in Kelly 1992:207)

Part of the problem is that prisons are seen in both professional and public discourse as a social necessity. A psychiatric worker explained:

> To me, for a child, it's kind of punitive but the community has to be protected. You have to balance the two issues; and some of the crimes that are committed are extremely violent, and there aren't resources in the youth system to deal with them.

The psychiatrist stated, "It's counter-productive to lock some kids up, but there are some kids that there is nothing you can do about; they are so bad." Incarceration, then, is perceived as a sensible solution to youth violence. Foucault's history of the origins of the modern prison explores this acceptance of the prison as an "obvious" or "natural" solution. "In a society which was already becoming inured to the operation of disciplinary mechanisms, the prison could appear to be self-evident right from the beginning" (Garland 1990:148).

A reliance on incarceration has contributed to the current trend towards transferring the most violent youths to adult prison. One psychiatric social worker indicated, "I've done more social history of transfer cases than any other social worker in the province and I have no hesitation [in recommending them]. It's perfectly right to face adult court and adult penalties, but there is a vast misunderstanding regarding the process"; he explained further that most often youths carry out their sentence in a youth facility until they turn eighteen. He also felt that "for certain offences youth sentences are not long enough, with the maximum penalty being only five years." The detective constable concurred: "We wholly agree; I mean a child knows what's right and wrong in varying degrees." He added: "There needs to be something for those who are too young to be affected by the YOA. They're untouchable until they turn twelve." He referred to the Bulger murder and a case where a ten-year-old was stealing up to thirty cars a week, knowing that he could not be charged until he was twelve. The authorities' support of transfer denies the context and experience of youths who reach that stage and ignores research that continually reaffirms the detrimental effects of encounters with hard-core prisoners (see Lipsey 1992).

Some authorities did not agree with transferring youths. One commented, "I do have trouble with that because they are in such flux; they're not on track yet, [and] they're not yet sure who they are. With transfer they are expected to know how serious what they're doing is." Kelly explains:

> It seems that, no matter the degree of conflict experienced by professionals—low level professionals in particular—and despite repeated acknowledgement of the blatant failure of the system at all levels of professional input, this still has no influence on the growth of a system which remains inherently resistant to improvement. (1992:207)

Sadly, reliance on incarceration produces some youths who idealize the institution and see their future in terms of a criminal career or a life of institutions. Dave, who is facing adult prison for murder, said:

> I agree with being transferred to adult, but I'm scared to go there because there's people there a lot bigger than me, and I'm really intimidated by them. I was thinking there should be an in-between jail for 18–25 years old just to get you ready for the big place.

Several youths indicated that they would prefer to spend their sentence in an adult prison. "I'd rather be in adult because time goes way quicker. I know lots of people there," said one. Ron agreed, "I'll ask to be transferred [because] adult is a lot better: better food, cleaner and they're not all immature like the punks here."

When I questioned the establishment authorities as to why some of the youths wanted to be transferred, several felt that "it is a lot of bravado." One probation officer reasoned, however, that workers in the youth system are expected to be doing something with the youths constantly.

So you're always in their face, trying to get them to do something—to go to school—and have activities for them and try and keep them going all the time, so they always have all this adult authority on them. And I think part [of their feeling] is that they can go to adult and they can be left alone; they think adult time is easier time.

However, according to a Foucauldian explanation, the youths' reaction is more a reflection of the fact that the prison "fabricates" delinquents.

It "made" delinquents in a literal sense by creating the conditions for recidivism: offenders were so stigmatized, demoralized, and deskilled in prison that after their release they tended to re-offend, to be reconvicted and eventually be transformed into career criminals. (Garland 1990:148)

The Agency of Youths

Smith (1987) argues that women have learned to deny their subjectivity and experience; so too have youth adapted to an alien discourse. Although youths generate their own discourse through language and practice, several of the youths' sentiments indicate the impact of "official knowledge" on their responses and, to an extent, the way in which it produces self-conscious subjects who perceive themselves through those official ways of thinking.

[T]he existence of rhetoric which emphasizes help and welfare whilst committing a child to a locked institution, and occasionally framing that action (conversely) as the fulfilment of a threat, can be expected to have consequences in terms of an inmate's construction of the "reality" of his or her situation once in the institution. (Kelly 1992:176)

The youths' ability to appropriate the languages and images of their captors is a central feature of their sense-making and self-empowering activities.

Reflecting on the official rationale for youth detention centres, a number of youths commented that the one good thing about being incarcerated is that it forces them to think. The OCP indicated that "for some kids incarceration is good [because] they're so out of control that it brings them to a standstill and gives them time to look at what they're doing." Katie proved this to be accurate:

I think about what happened a lot and I'm grateful that I came here. I've fought about five times in two months because I just like to start them and if I didn't come here I just wonder what if something more serious would have happened. I wouldn't want that. I think I'll be at a different mental level when I get out, and I won't see fighting as natural anymore. But now that I'm wasting nineteen months of my life and it came so close to that girl not living, I now have that little second in my mind that says this isn't worth it.

This illustrates that "the experience of being incarcerated is clearly anxiety-provoking, but is generally presented to children by authorities and by staff in the unit as helpful and rehabilitative" (Kelly 1992:177). However, in the same breath, Katie claimed, "But if someone comes running at me, I will fight, but I won't provoke them." This illustrates that, despite good intentions, the reality of the youths' experiences are often incongruent with official expectation. Obviously their experiences deny the institution's attempt to create the impression of organization, coherence and objectivity (Kelly 1992:104).

Similarly, some youths commented that change in behaviour comes only from within. A probation officer recognized this:

I think the programs work for some kids, and other kids are just ready to quit. If you're forced by your PO to go to anger management and you think it's a joke and you don't want to be there, you're not going to get much out of it.

Jane said, "This place isn't going to change you; you change yourself. You have to want to change." She described the various programs she was in but said that whether or not they are helpful "depends on what kind of person you are, and whether you want it. Like I've had enough of it; I'm not going back to that way.... I can't."

Kelly (1992) argues that the attitudes of youths towards staff and the institution—approval, dependence, submission, hostility—survive in competition with the most widely held belief that change and staying out of trouble are independent processes over which the individual has the real control. The attitude of youth is changed, however, by positive contact with staff, which fragments the very real experience of adversarial power relations (Kelly 1992:180). Dave was very positive about the various programs and felt that he had "learned a lot," but he also remarked, "I benefit because I want to benefit.... The psychologists say that three years is great; it will be enough time to rehabilitate me, and that means that I'll only do a year [in adult prison]." Kelly (1992:206) extrapolates from Edelman (1977): "language and attitude of staff blurred the recognition of adversary interests by present staff as helping and rehabilitative. The result was confusion and a greater probability of compliance on the part of inmates."

Some of the youths pointed out what the criminological literature recognizes as the classic detriment of being incarcerated. "What makes it worse is when you just come in and out and become institutionalized; you get out and you want to come back in," Ron commented. "I have goals on the outs; I try to meet those goals, but a fight will fuck everything up." Alex claimed, "This place is hurtin' [and] you learn more stuff like how to do crime in here. They should have some kind of program 'cause this place just makes you worse; it makes you institutionalized." Overall, the incongruity of real experience and official rhetoric often provokes anxiety in inmates. "The ambivalence of the situation renders it unpredictable—uncontrollable; access to real information is prevented by the creation of a smokescreen of individual and mystifictory treatment rationales" (Kelly 1992:177).

The conflict between youth and establishment authority is prominent at every stage of the youth justice system. Once again, the disjuncture stems from an ignorance or dismissal of the youths' experience of the system. Although their perspective is often disregarded, the youths are not passive participants. They both resist and appropriate professional discourse to make sense of their experience. For example, the youths' refusal to lie in court, on the advice of the lawyers who are technically there to help them, is ironic (and naive from an adult perspective) but empowering. The youths' reference to being "institutionalized" or "rehabilitated" is also part of their sense-making. This is explained by Wright-Mills' (1959) notion of the "vocabulary of motive," which recognizes that "whatever the accessible cultural rationale is, we borrow it to explain ourselves. We use the vocabulary when we know it's not the truth, and we use it when we don't know what the truth is" (cited in Pearson 1997:40). There is the obviously negative effect when youths live up to their captors' expectations and begin to see their life in terms of a criminal career. Unfortunately, from the youths' perspective, there is little done within the institution to prevent them from committing more crime. Nowhere is the disjuncture in perspectives more destructive than in the philosophy behind programming the violent offender. An emphasis on anger management negates the youths' reality both inside and outside of prison. Rather than recognizing the value youths place on respect and reputation, which signify group dynamics, the authorities continue to focus on individual personality. These ideas for reform do not offer much hope.

The Future

The youths had diverse outlooks on their future. At one end of the spectrum was the prospect of adult prison and at the other was the dream of becoming a doctor. Youths who hope for a life outside of prison face tremendous obstacles upon release. Life in the youth detention centre does little to prepare them for life on the outside. Much of this section details the authorities' perception of how to deal with the problem. Their resistance to challenging professional understanding is evident in their continual reliance on anger management as the main solution. While the youths' recognition of structural solutions is ignored, the authorities' response has rendered lost the most violent youths.

Impossible Dreams

The youths' future aspirations were diverse but, without recognition and help in overcoming the structural barriers they will undoubtedly face when they get out, there is little hope that their dreams will be realized. The girls in particular wanted to work with kids like themselves. "I want to major in Crim. and Psych. and work with people like me," Katie said. "I wish there was a way to know beforehand that a kid was going to grow up violent, so that people could go in there and help the kid out." Jane wants to be a doctor. Other youths were less optimistic about the future. When asked what he wanted to do when he left Willingdon Mark stated tongue-in-cheek, "Get in a car accident and break my lower back so I can sit in a wheelchair so I can't do anything wrong anymore. I can live off insurance, and I won't have to do crime."

Knowing what the youths' aspirations were, I inquired into how the authorities would assist them in accomplishing their goals. All establishment authorities agreed that some form of programming aimed specifically at violent youths is necessary, but few had any idea of what that should entail. Unlike the youths, most authorities suggested a simple expansion or improvement of existing programs. As Kelly correctly notes, "professionals have become the hub of the system, creating its rhetoric, defining its objectives, justifying its failure and generating new areas of influence" (1992:34).

These "new areas of influence" illustrate that the medical model is extremely powerful in justifying social control (Kelly 1992:171). One of the psychiatric social workers who ran anger management groups acknowledged that the program does "not address everything about violence [and that] there is a need for a more comprehensive approach." He commented that "any programming would have to be multiphasic and have more institutional backing." I asked the director about the vision of a new program aimed at violent offenders, and his outline incorporated everything I have been critical of up to this point, including an emphasis on the medical "treatment" and classification of "sick" youths, which rationalizes violent behaviour as an individual problem. He explained that a new program would expand anger management into a "multi-system," which would incorporates three areas. The first area would be group therapy to deal with the youths' impulsive behaviour, Attention Deficit Hyperactivity Disorder (ADHD) and avoidance of conflict. Treatment would include medication and would target youths considered reactive aggressive individuals; instrumental violent individuals, he explained, may not be accepted into the new program because of severe psychopathy. The second area would be family therapy, including group homes. It would address pathology in the family and issues of neglect and abuse and would focus on the best ways for caregivers to deal with violent behaviour.

The third area would not include a therapeutic component but would offer a way to enforce youth participation in the completion of the program. Probation officers would include the program as a condition of probation and charge the youths with breach of probation when they fail to attend. The director explained that this condition is essential because "the time factor is a major problem in the sense of out of sight, out of mind." It is believed that unless the youths are coerced into attending the program and punished for failing to do so, they will resist treatment. The new program would be conducted as out-patient treatment, he indicated. Expanding anger management into an organizing principle of an entire institution is an example of Cohen's (1985) classification systems. Although these systems may be demonstrably inefficient in terms of "reha-bilitating" violent youths, the classification systems "reinforce the control systems which they seem bound to undermine; in fact, they serve to elaborate the system's field of influence" (Kelly 1992:104).

Public anxiety over youth crime is reduced by the argument that psychology, psychiatry and medicine will "treat" violent offenders. Public acceptance reinforces the continual use of anger management. Yet, one of the psychiatric social workers identified a current problem with anger management—insufficient time to treat the offender: "There needs to be an awareness in the community that you need a period of time." Edelman (1977:67) notes:

> [T]he lay public by and large adopts the professional perspective; for its major concern is to believe that others can be trusted to handle these problems, which are potentially threatening to them but not part of their everyday lives. This public reaction is the politically crucial one, for it confers power on professionals and spreads their norms to others. (cited in Kelly 1992:172)

Thus, it is evident that anger management is justified in the professional discourse and is, in a covert sense, supported by the public. The fact that the director's idea for expanding anger management is a "vision" of things to come and that there appears to be little public resistance to it offers little hope that youths will overcome structural realities and realize success in the future.

Prevention Strategies Create a Lost Group of "Individuals"

The authorities' perception of violent youths as an inherently violent group is incompatible with the youth respondents' view of themselves as having individual worth; it also stifles the search for alternatives and a fresh start for young offenders upon their release. Those who focus on youths' "inherent" violence and high risk of recidivism see few options beyond prison for this "lost group," and so they focus their resources on community-level and particularly family-level prevention. This strategy also focuses attention on individual as opposed to structural factors and could potentially direct the blame for youth delinquency at parents. The psychiatrist was a proponent of this view: we must "focus on prevention: a way to deal with people who have kids and issues of neglect and giving the kids too much freedom."

The detective constable, reflecting police philosophy in general, also supported prevention through school and the family. This belief in the ability to detect "pre-delinquency" (Schissel 1993:9 cited in Schissel 1997:54) is an indictment of families, particularly single mothers. When one assumes criminality and immorality to be the product of poor parenting, poverty and single-motherhood there is no recognition of economic and social structures as causes of youth hostility (Schissel 1997:54, 66). Such generalizations "are most damaging in that they neglect to contextualize crime problems within a social structure in which people are given privilege on the bases of wealth, prestige, race and gender" (Schissel 1997:69). Additional harm results when the belief that society needs to be vigilant for signs of criminality translates prevention strategies into policing the marginalized.

> [O]ne of the risks in advocating programs that deal with crime, deviance and dispossession is that we may be fostering more social control over already disenfranchised youth. And this is possible if school programs, for example, become so intrusive into the personal and psychic lives of youths that they become violators of human rights. (Schissel 1997:116)

Attempts to incorporate prevention at the community level "widens the net" of social control and ignores the realities of violent youths. For example, the constable, in looking at ways to deal with youth through the community, explained:

> [An individual at the] Hastings Community Centre is trying to start something at the grass-roots level that is similar to a healing circle [in which] the young person is committed with his/her parents and the penalty is set out within a group with community representatives.

However, as Harris and Webb (1987) argue, in a superficial sense, the spread of evermore imaginative and inclusive community corrections embraces a wide range of social punishments.

> [T]he current diversifications include a set of technologies designed to address and control the apparently criminogenic aspects of mind, body, and social situation ... a restructuring of the institution by the creation and development of a set of middle-range correctional strategies designed precisely to break down the divide between community and institution. (Harris and Webb 1987:161–62)

Thus, there is greater penetration and surveillance at the community level while structural inequities within communities remain unaddressed (Kelly 1992:207). In keeping with a Left Realist approach, Schissel (1997) argues that state policy can reduce discrimination and injustice for youth offenders, notwithstanding the existence of social stratification and patriarchy. It must honour the importance of individual responsibility but, at the same time, ensure that the wider community attempts to address the injustices inherent in stratified society (Schissel 1997:109).

The newly created British Columbia Ministry of Child and Family Services reflects legislative change focused on prevention, but it does not address the need, as Schissel (1997) recommends, to recognize structural inequalities. The one judge I interviewed had conducted an inquiry into the five ministries that deal with children and youth: Social Services; Attorney General; Education; Health; and Women's Equality. The judge's main conclusion was that, because the ministries did not share their information with one another, the system was failing those whom it was designed to serve: "It's unrealistic and ineffective to treat young people at age twelve in an isolated department; it's part of a larger problem of children and families, and that's the way it should be dealt with." Based on the judge's condemnation of the separate ministries, there was an amalgamation of all five ministries. He claimed:

[Although] some bureaucrats and union leaders do not agree [with the change], there is no one that actually does the work that does not agree that one organization should assume responsibility for the provision of services to children and youth.... It's going to significantly improve the quality of services to young people.... [I]t will assist in rehabilitation and reduce recidivism because fewer kids will be pushed out the door of correction facilities with no support.

On the recommendation of the judge, I interviewed the local director of the new youth services division for Burnaby to find out more about the "team" that deals with young offenders. He explained that the current model includes about eighteen positions: five probation officers, one to deal with sex offenders at Youth Court Services and four to deal with the Burnaby caseload; five social workers, one of whom is responsible for information for court hearings, four of whom deal with child protection issues and three of whom manage the entire caseload of youths aged twelve and over who are in foster care; one resource person to oversee office and administration matters, such as finding new foster homes; two mental health workers, usually a psychiatrist and a psychologist for therapy sessions; one drug and alcohol worker to serve a community function; and a special counsellor connected to the school system. According to the judge, the goal of these integrated services "is to prevent so many kids from falling through the cracks."

The stereotypical view of violent youths and other realities of the system may prevent youth from benefitting from this amalgamation. I asked some of the other authorities for their opinion of the new ministry. The OCP indicated:

I hope that we'll see some real changes, but I'm not sure that these kids will benefit. I don't think we'll be very high on the priority list [because] there are so many other things in the community that they'll focus on first. I hope I'm wrong. There is a whole community of kids here with a lot of needs.

One of the probation officers was similarly sceptical.

We'll see when the dollars go into prevention, and right now we're in a deficit situation; so ironically there's no money for new programs, but we're setting up a new ministry. When they start throwing money into prevention that's when we'll start looking seriously at changing the way we think; it needs to be done in a big way.

Once again, authorities who had the most contact with the youths seemed realistic about professional rhetoric. They also appeared to have few options in such a structured system of hierarchy. In explanation, Haines (1996:207) draws on Giddens' (1990) connections between trust and risk:

> [I]ndividuals, at every level of the organisation, are forced to place trust in the validity (and security) of organisational policies and procedures such that what they do will be complemented by the actions of others, and that by virtue of nothing one does directly, the whole system continues to function and does not fall apart. (Haines 1996:207)

Although great effort and resources are put into prevention, this approach continues to ignore violent youths already incarcerated. As one of the judges explained, the most violent youths are those who "fall through the cracks" in the sense that their violent history becomes entrenched. He stated that he is a "big fan" of wilderness programs:

> [T]here are young people that could benefit from that program but don't fit into it because their violent behaviour poses such a risk.... I mean you can't have kids running around with axes if they have real anger management problems.

The judge is implying that violence, as an inherent part of the youths' personality, will be prevalent in all circumstances. This ignores the youths' view that their violence occurred as isolated acts in specific situations. Nevertheless, their violent tendencies disqualify them from innovative programming. For example, a document in Andrea's file recommended that her incarceration be followed by placement in the Vernon Women's Transition House Program. The response was that the "Vernon Program will not accept [Andrea] given her history of arson and assaultive behaviours." In general, the judge concluded: "Those who are most needy are put into institutional facilities where their behaviour is monitored and [where it] is safer for them and other residents, but they're not getting the benefit [of innovative programs]." Youths who end up in Willingdon are distinguished less by the complexity of their needs and more by the fact that they are not easily absorbed into other resources in the youth justice system.

The traditional attitude that "nothing works" with this group of youths has resulted in lengthy periods of incarceration as the only sentencing option. Although some establishment authorities had ideas for other programs, the responses generally did not challenge the ideology of the institution nor consider the youths' perspectives. For this reason I asked the youths what they thought would work best if they could design the programs.

Recognizing Structural Barriers in Alternatives after Release

Upon release, youths return to a society antagonistic to their needs. The number of American children living in poverty increased by 2.2 million nationwide between 1979 and 1989, and the trend continues (Giroux 1996:206). Giroux contends:

> [D]espite endless rhetoric about "family values" and "protecting our children," the wealthiest and most powerful forces in our society have demonstrated by their actions that they feel that young people do not matter, that they can be our nation's lowest priority. (1996:206)

From tax cuts that ignore pressing needs to the imposition of huge debts upon and disinvestment in schools, our young people are bearing the brunt of the greed of a small group of wealthy adults. Even more detrimental is how being poor and young translates into blame. In 1996, the British Columbia government reduced welfare provisions to young people in support of mandatory job searches on the assumption that there is work if idle youths want it (Schissel 1997:66–67). As Giroux recognizes, youths not only face the consequences of economic downsizing, they often find themselves being regulated within institutions that have little relevance to their lives (1996:13). In light of these conditions, and the pressures of consumerism aimed at youth, as outlined in Chapter Three, the future is dismal for the average youth and even more so for those discharged from a detention centre with no supports.

It is not surprising, therefore, that youths say that having a job upon release would be the most helpful means of preventing future crime. "Try to help them get a job," said Josh. "If you have a job, that takes most of your time away." Alex had spent time at Boulder Bay camp and said, "It's a good place to be [because] it's just like a work camp. I had a full-time kitchen job there; having a job helps." One of the judges agreed, stating that he was tired of the public complaining about youth violence but not doing anything about it. He suggested that we need someone to challenge the public to set up community-based programs and, in particular, to marshall resources from the business community. Because both youths and authorities recognize a lack of self-esteem among young offenders, the judge suggested support for when they get out. A probation officer also agreed: "Overall, if you want to change the behaviour of a kid, it's the same for all: try and get them a job, and to stay in school."

Several youths commented on the need for alternative housing and new environments once they are released. As Clint said, "A lot of these guys get out and go back to the same friends; they need to go to completely different environments." Once the tape-recorder was turned off, Jane discussed more about prostitution, explaining that girls have nowhere to go once they are released. Housing alternatives for these youths do not exist. As the OCP at Willingdon stated:

> I think it's the transition back to the community that needs to be looked at; that's where we really fall down. I would really like to see these kids released to half-way houses where they are with people who would be helping them use their skills. Lots of the kids leave really not wanting to come back, but there's nobody to help them. How, for example, do they get a job? We recognize that adults need that kind of thing, but we don't for youth. There are foster homes and transition workers, but the kids are still in homes that are dysfunctional and workers aren't there all the time.

The psychiatric social worker, who is in charge of the sex offender treatment programs, indicated that because the problem of violence has become more serious, there are more difficulties finding resources: "Caregivers have to have a different set of skills because these guys have horrendous records, [and] they're very intimidating. It's a whole new challenge housing them."

It is inconceivable how the challenges associated with innovative programming are judged, by the authorities, to be more risky than sending a "violent youth" back to the community with no support systems. It is also hard to comprehend how the youths' common-sense solutions, such as help in finding a job or housing, are not part of any current plans for reform. The youths clearly state that a large part of their criminal activity is a result of their monetary needs, which again echo the emphasis in critical criminology on structural obstacles that contribute to crime. The pressure to live up to the materialistic standards presented in the media is impossible to do on a legitimate basis for youths who have no jobs. This is seldom recognized by the authorities; when it is acknowledged, the youths' motives are questioned or their personality "type" disqualifies them from innovative programs.

Conclusion

After listening to fifteen youths describe their history of criminal acts and their experiences in youth detention centres, and knowing that they are only a small percentage of the young offender population, I can understand how the "nothing works" mindset of several academics filters down to those who design and implement policy. As Schissel (1997:166) recognizes, "this pessimism is not only counterproductive but dangerous because it generates an apathy among public officials and youth workers that provokes ineptitude." Rather than chancing innovative reform, the response, as recognized by Foucault (1979), has typically been to build more prisons even though their detrimental effects are understood. Describing prisons as a "societal necessity" is often the justification for doing so.

This study is an attempt by yet another researcher to explore an alternative approach. The last two chapters have detailed the perspectives of both authorities and youths in their own words. And it is obvious that most of our difficulties in understanding violence, in portraying violence in the media in a less sensational way and in devising solutions to the problem of youth violence stem in part from the fact that the voice of youth is not used to produce knowledge, inform policy and reform programs. Youths in general signify an awkward age that is not easily definable. The result of falling somewhere between an independent child with no rights and a responsible adult who is fully accountable is alienation and injustice. For this reason part of the solution to youth violence must include empowering the dispossessed. Schissel argues it is this basic premise that has resulted in successful programming elsewhere:

> In [his book] *Last One Over the Wall*, Jerome Miller (1991), the former commissioner of the Massachusetts Department of Youth Services, describes how he closed down the state's reform schools for young offenders, beginning with maximum security young inmates. The alternatives offered were based on community care, specifically community homes for young offenders, and former carceral resources were devoted to community prevention programs that provided improved education and work opportunities for underprivileged youth. After two decades, despite concerted and constant political pressure to reopen youth prisons, Massachusetts locks up fewer teenagers than any other state, its recidivism rates have dropped dramatically, the number of adult inmates who were alumni of the youth system have fallen by half.... All of this occurred with no increased risk to public safety. (1997:117)

There are other examples of non-punitive restorative approaches to youth justice such as Maori-based "family group conferencing" in New Zealand or preventative high school programs in Saskatoon, but the fundamental principle behind the success of all such programs is to provide youths with the opportunity to make choices and to create an "adultlike world in which autonomy, responsibility, respect and enfranchisement are the cornerstones" (Schissel 1997:123). When punishment and imposed authority are replaced with mutual input and respect, youths, even those with violent tendencies, have a much greater chance of responding positively.

Chapter Five

Conclusions
"Tainted Personalities" Mask Youths' Reality

The overall finding of this study is that the disjuncture between the perspective of youths and that of establishment authority on the issue of youth violence is significant and has wide-reaching ramifications for the young violent offender. The social relations that inform this disjuncture are revealed through a Foucauldian understanding of "knowledge" and how it is both relational to and reflective of positions of power. The result is that the official word on and public view of youth violence consider it a personal pathology that should be addressed as such. The establishment authorities' treatment of violent youths as "tainted personalities" ignores the youths' experience and understanding of their violence. It is evident that the silencing of youths in popular culture, the media and the justice system stems in part from one of the main creators of ideology: academia. Here is where the challenge to change the situation must also begin. It has been the intent of this study to convey the importance of a new perspective on and approach to studying and appreciating the standpoint of violent youths.

An analysis of the disjuncture between youths and establishment authority clearly illustrates Foucault's (1980) notion that knowledge is relational. Although knowledge is often accepted as "objective" because it is presented by experts, it is in fact created and reflective of time, place and the perspective of those in positions of power. Historical studies have mapped the changing modes of social control that have unfolded over the years, and it is obvious that the panic over violent youths reflects larger societal issues. In fact, Schissel (1997) states that the phenomenon of children-blaming is historically common. In the seventeenth century, for example, children were perceived as a social problem. He cites a passage about life in an English town during this period and observes:

> [I]t is remarkable how much it echoes the alarmist rhetoric in contemporary Canadian media and political accounts: the inherent danger of children, their particularly pathological vulnerability to alcohol, the importance of household discipline and "family values," and the "problem" of poverty and the reluctance of youth to become involved in wage labour. (Schissel 1997:114)

Interestingly, this list also echoes the sentiments of both the academics writing about youth violence (see Chapter One) and the perceptions of the adult respondents in this study.

The process of knowledge production reflects, in Smith's (1987) words, the "relations of ruling" which are integral to understanding the current discourses on youth violence.

> Foucault argues that historical periods are marked by particular discourses that constrain the types of knowledge produced. Within historical periods, knowledge is constructed and deployed on the basis of what types of people have access to systems of knowledge, and it is this access to "legitimate knowledge" that gives people their power. (Schissel 1997:105)

Discourse is derived from the language of "legitimated speakers," who define the rules under which "talk" can be carried out. Thus, the discourse on youth violence has produced "truths" that are reflective of those from the privileged sectors of society. "The growing focus on criminogenic children ... diverts public debate away from the political actions of the powerful that create social stresses for the less powerful (unemployment, welfare-state cuts, dangerous work environment, poorly paid and part-time labour)" (Schissel 1997:16).

The result of professional discourse is to restrict accounts of violent youth to individual blame, with no recognition of structural injustices. "The producers of the message implicitly suggest that crime is a matter of inherent evil that is manifested in deviant ... behaviour" (Schissel 1997:35). It is understandable that those from Youth Court Services, who are trained in psychological assessment and counselling, would comment from a psychological perspective, but I was surprised that police officers, probation officers and even judges criticized young offenders on the basis of their purportedly flawed personalities. The characterization and categorization of personality types were simply accepted without challenge.

Although the term "tainted personality" was not used by any of the establishment authorities, I think it signifies their belief that violent youths are outside the bounds of normality. The effect of classifying violent youths as a group with inherent defects is that they are objectified and treated accordingly. For example, several times throughout the interviews, establishment authorities referred to the youths as "dysfunctional," implying that such deficiencies are an intrinsic part of their being. There were other characterizations, such as their liking violent music and movies and their "vicious" or untrustworthy attributes, which suggest that violent youths constitute a personality-disordered class. The assumption of gang connections and the police reliance on "no contact orders" illustrate the authorities' belief that youths become "tainted" by association with other personality-flawed youths.

Nowhere is the authorities' emphasis on "tainted personality" more evident than in the philosophy behind programming. Because violent youths are perceived as deviant, they fall outside the realm of "normal" treatment. The consequence is often that, because the youths are supposedly inherently violent, there is "no hope" and therefore no programs available. For example, the overwhelming emphasis on prevention implies that once youths commit a violent offence, they are "beyond the pale" and incapable of change. Such a focus also ignores countless studies (see for example Snyder and Sickmund 1995; Schissel 1993, 1997) that indicate that very few youths commit multiple, serious offences. And when it comes to the issue of community protection, it is assumed that, because of inherent and seemingly immutable traits, these youths will re-offend. The frequent response of medical practitioners, including those at YCS, is to administer drugs to control abnormal personality characteristics.

The problem with the authorities' perception is that it does not correspond to the experience of youths. The youths say their violent actions are particular to the circumstances and have no bearing on their personality. They see their crimes as isolated events rather than the result of who they are. Moreover, youths perceive a double standard in the sense that, from where they stand, the adult world seems equally, if not more, violent than their own. The media also portray the youths as having tainted personalities, but it must be acknowledged that adults, including the establishment authorities, are the main consumers of such "information." The recycling of stereotypes legitimizes official ways of knowing. The interpretation of youth violence is made by authorities; it is reiterated by the media, often in a sensational context; and then it is fed back to authorities as truth, reinforced and sanctioned by adult public opinion.

Hence, a large part of the conflict stems from the experience and status of being an adult or that of a child. The confusion over how to deal with violent youths is reflected in the contradictory measures taken by the justice system. On the one hand, authorities impose childhood standards on youths, which enforces the idea that they are without responsibilities and rights. On the other hand, the youths are forced to deal with and address a level of violence within carceral institutions that is inconsistent with their status as children. The incongruence was recognized by one youth who questioned how he could be tried in an adult court and do adult time but not be considered adult enough to buy alcohol. "The child is the modern prototypical scapegoat, forced to live in an adult world without the rights and abilities to influence and shape that world and to defend his or her rights" (Schissel 1997:116).

Throughout this study, I have heard several authority figures describe work in the field of youth justice as "frustrating." I think this signifies the constraints operating against efforts by authorities to make positive reforms within a static establishment. Although the bulk of my analysis entails a condemnation of establishment authority for their role in the silencing of youths, this conclusion must be understood within a wider context. My criticisms are directed at a correctional system based on long-standing relations of ruling rather than at the individuals who are, often unknowingly, an integral element of those relations. This study is in no way meant to undermine the work, sincerity or dedication of the establishment authorities interviewed. Their desire for and commitment to making a better life for violent youths were evident in most interviews. In fact, several authorities indicated a genuine concern and affection for the youths. Moreover, all of the establishment authorities expressed an interest in my research and acknowledged the need for alternatives in dealing with violent youths.

Academic theorizing is often criticized as unrealistic by practitioners at the front-lines of youth justice. Just as I have criticized authorities for ignoring the perspective of youths' lived experience, it is often the case that grand theorizing ignores the realities of those expected to implement the ideas. For example, several authorities commented on how desensitized they are to extreme forms of violence because they see and deal with it on a daily basis. It should not be surprising that the frustrations of seeing the same youths pass through "the revolving door" result in an inability to appreciate their perspective on anything. In addition, the devastation and harm that result from acts of violence cannot be understated. The sentiment that the "monsters" who commit these acts do not deserve the recognition I am suggesting is understandable from the perspective of someone who has suffered as a result. It is much easier to punish the "folk devils," with whom we do not empathize (Schissel 1997). Nonetheless, academic suggestions of new possibilities, however unrealistic, spark reaction, debate and eventually change.

Allowing youths a voice in matters that directly affect them is a starting point for change. At no point in the study have I thought or suggested that young people should be afforded the decision-making power of adults. However, youths are disenfranchised from the democratic process at levels of governance. Increasing punishment to appease our "moral panic" will result in the "alienation of a more uncompromising and disaffiliated youth population" (Schissel 1997:10). Including their perspective in decisions made about their lives can only be constructive. By nature, people of any age group will respond more positively to self-initiated solutions than to those which are imposed from outside authority. Recognizing the importance of the youth perspective may be the beginning of reforming how we treat violent offenders. More than asking their opinion, we must respect their responses. As in the case of women, it is time for us to appreciate young people as "knowers" of their own situation.

This book emphasizes the benefit derived from a new approach to the study of youth violence. There is a considerable body of knowledge in mainstream criminology that informs the discourse on youth violence. It is not my intent to discredit all of the existing work but to recognize the severe limitations of such a one-sided approach. In particular, I want to draw attention to a different source of knowledge as yet untapped and to value the knowledge of children. Smith (1987) clearly understood the benefit of allowing women's voices to prevail, which has changed human understanding on numerous issues. As was the case with emerging feminism, it will no doubt be difficult to change the ideals that justify the marginalization of young people. It is a challenge not only to societal understanding of the status of young people but to the discourse of criminology itself.

Appendix I

Summary of Youth Respondents

Alex (age 17)
Alex was an Aboriginal youth described by the OCP as suffering from fetal alcohol syndrome. He was aggressive both inside and outside of the institution and had been in foster homes most of his life. Although he claimed his mom was always there for him, he admitted that she was an alcoholic. Alex was sentenced to ten months incarceration after he and his friend beat another youth for "ratting them out." It was obvious in the interview that he had not either thought about or not formed an opinion on several of the questions I asked. It was evident, however, that he disliked almost everything about the institution.

Andrea (age 17)
Andrea had an extensive record of offences, including harassment/stalking, intimidation, and being unlawfully at large. Her most recent charge was for assault with a weapon. She beat up and cut another female youth with a knife for "ratting" on her best friend. The incident went on throughout the night, and the police tried to charge Andrea with forceable confinement. She was sentenced to a year-long term of incarceration. She had a good relationship with her mom but said that her dad was an alcoholic who beat her (and she beat him). She continually ran away from home and lived on the streets of downtown Toronto for a while. During the interview, I sensed that she enjoyed the attention of someone listening to her. In addition, she was perhaps hoping for "shock value" from some of her responses; she volunteered information that was not in keeping with the discussion and she would use swear words whenever possible. For example, in response to displeasure with a staff member's reaction Andrea stated, "so I kicked him in the bu… ass."

Clint (age 18)
Clint had been charged only with property offences until after his incarceration. He was charged with assault in Willingdon after beating up another youth who had scattered his magazines down the hallway. Clint explained that he had to establish himself so that the other inmates would no longer take advantage of him. He claimed that he had a fairly

good relationship with his parents "but not on a prolonged basis." In the interview Clint was extremely articulate and well versed in institutional and clinical language. In fact, he described his life like a case study: up until age six he was "a perfect little angel"; the grief over the death of his grandma started his delinquent behaviour at age seven, which contributed to his parents' divorce. He then became the only "criminally-minded" person in his group of friends and always "took the fall for the guys." He stated that the programs in Willingdon were not effective, and he had prepared a list of "how resources could be changed and made better ... by the perspective of someone who has gone through the programs." This comment may have been prompted by my consent form which, because he was eighteen, he signed himself.

Daryl (age 18)

Among numerous property charges, Daryl also had committed unlawful confinement and assault with a weapon after escaping from prison in the Northwest Territories. He and his accomplice broke into the house of a man who came home while the youths were still inside. The youths put a gun to the man's head and made him drive them out of town. The man escaped at a gas station and called the police; the youths were caught on the other side of town. Daryl then escaped on foot and hid in an abandoned house. Confused by what was happening, Daryl grabbed a towel rack, walked to the neighbour's house, rang the door bell and, as he explained, "whoever answered the door, I smacked them and walked away." He was sentenced to three years in a Northwest Territories detention centre. His most recent sentence was for car theft, possession of stolen property, two B&Es and being unlawfully at large. He remembered that there had been a lot of drinking and abuse while he was growing up, and he claimed that his dad could "get violent." He also thought that a lot of his problems stemmed from the people he "hung out with." Daryl appeared agitated throughout the interview. He made little eye contact, did not express any positive emotion and was non-responsive to some questions. He explained at the end of the interview that he was "freakin' out" because he needed something, either drugs or counselling, to deal with the recent death of a friend.

Dave (age 18)

Dave was incarcerated for manslaughter after he and four of his friends tried to rob a drunk man who was walking down the street. The man refused to hand over his wallet so the youths beat him. They had no intention of killing him. The group heard over the news that the man had died. Dave claimed that they had a couple of beers and had smoked some pot but that they all knew what they were doing at the time of the incident.

Dave was tricked into a confession. The case went through a series of trials and Dave was raised to adult court. At the time of the interview he had been in Willingdon for seven months awaiting his trial. Since being incarcerated, he beat up another youth who was in for sexual assault because "we frown upon that kind of stuff." He explained that there was a lot of violence in his family and he remembered that, when he was quite young, his dad used to "pound" his mom. Dave appeared very settled within Willingdon and found comfort in the routine.

Ed (age 18)
Ed was on probation at the time of the interview. Although he had been involved in a robbery with his friends, he received the lesser charge of assault in exchange for pleading guilty. The group needed money so they walked into a store with machetes and "held up" the cashier. Ed was "on the look-out" and no violence was involved. He had previous trafficking and car theft charges. Ed had a good home and he recognized that his parents were doing everything they could to keep him from committing more crime. Ed claimed that a lot of his friends were Vietnamese youths who came from a tough country and had to commit crime because they had no support in Canada. Ed was Chinese and claimed that, due to racism, police single out Asian youths as deviant. He was very shy at the beginning of the interview and did not elaborate much. However, by the time I drove him to his court appearance, he was openly discussing the techniques of auto theft and his desire to travel around the United States working on electrical repairs with his uncle.

Garth (age 15)
Garth claimed that much of his criminal behaviour stemmed from needing money for his substance addictions. His list of offences included: two B&Es; dangerous driving; two charges of possession of stolen property; robberies; and breaches of probation orders. He did not describe himself as a violent person, but he did have an assault charge for "beating the crap" out of a guy. He and his sister had been sexually abused by their mom's boyfriend, who was not charged because "he beat a lie-detector test." Garth had spent a lot of time running away from home when he was younger but said that he had been getting along with his mother recently and had become a father also. Although he claimed that his son was his motivation to "quit crime," it was evident during the interview that his experience in the system and his maturity level may prevent him from doing so. At the time of the interview, he was charging the police with brutality for a beating he received during an arrest.

Summary of Youth Respondents

Graham (age 18)
Graham had a lengthy record of possession of stolen property, car theft and break-and-enter. He had been charged with a robbery, during which he and a friend pulled a knife on two kids in a parking lot and demanded money. He also had an assault charge for joining a group of his friends in "stomping" another youth. He was most recently incarcerated on a mischief charge, brought against him after his fingerprints were found on a car he had stolen three years previously. Graham had "done time" earlier in Willingdon, several wilderness camps and adult prison. He described his home life as good, although his mother had a bad drug habit. He had a job at the time of his arrest but feared he would lose it, having been incarcerated. He appeared amazingly calm throughout the interview considering the circumstance, but he responded to several questions with "I don't know," making little attempt to elaborate.

Jane (age 16)
Jane was sentenced to thirty-eight months for her role in the killing of her pimp. She got involved in a prostitution ring when she was fourteen years old. Jane explained that her co-accused had threatened her life if she did not participate in the murder. She was terrified of (and in love with) her pimp, who also threatened to kill her. Jane explained that she was stuck in the woods in the middle of the night, drinking with her two co-accused. The older one had planned the murder, which Jane claimed she did not really know about at the time. When the pimp arrived, the three girls beat him and then drowned him in the nearby creek. Jane said that she had been a happy child but went "down hill" around age four or five when her parents got divorced. She was close to her father but had been forced to live with her mother with whom she did not get along. Jane stated that her mom beat her. Jane's charge of possession of a deadly weapon resulting from threatening her mom with a knife because she was scared. Jane appeared to be timid at the beginning of the interview, which was partially my fault in that I had no time to be "briefed" about what she had done. She was reluctant to discuss her involvement and commented several times, "This is hard for me." Obviously she was sensitive to being judged negatively by people who did not understand the circumstances. Once she felt comfortable that I was not there to judge her, she described the realities of being a prostitute and said she was relieved knowing her pimp was dead.

Josh (age 18)
Josh had been part of several gangs and had committed various crimes as a result. During the time of the interview he was in Willingdon on an extortion charge because he and his friend threatened to shoot another

127

youth if he did not pay them $800. Josh's previous extortion charge occurred during a similar situation, but it resulted in "a severe beating": he and six other guys kicked down the victim's front door, beat him and his brother and trashed their house. Josh recognized that it was good that his family had not given up on him, and his deterrent to future crime was the fact that he did not want an adult record. A problem in accomplishing this perhaps would be his loyalty to "friends," which was expressed several times in the interview.

Katie (age 15)
Katie was a temporary ward of the state. She grew up with "bikers" and described her home life as "violent." She had a lengthy history of assault, breaches, possession of stolen property, possession of an illegal firearm and breaking-and-entering. She was serving a nineteen-month sentence for aggravated assault and uttering threats to cause death or bodily harm. Her co-accused included her older sister and another youth. All three girls had severely beat another young female. Katie was described by the OCP as bright and mature, which rang true in the interview. She wanted to go to Simon Fraser University and major in criminology and psychology upon her release.

Mark (age 17)
Mark had been convicted of assault with a weapon after he and his brother beat their mother's previous boyfriend with ski-poles. He was released on bail and had since been incarcerated for beating up his friend. The incident occurred while Mark was drunk. He described his home life as "dysfunctional." He had been involved in several property offences and thought he should be in adult prison because "time goes way quicker." He claimed not to miss his freedom because all he did when he was out was "make money, get stoned and party." During the interview Mark expressed a lot of frustration with both the system and himself. He acknowledged several times that his anger built up until he lost control.

Ron (age 17)
Ron was incarcerated for assault charges after he and his friends went to a party on a First Nations reserve. A fight involving several people broke out, and Ron "smashed" a guy's head with a bumper-jack, giving him a compound fracture. Ron was initially charged with attempted murder. He was also charged with assaults on two other people at the party. Ron claimed that he did not go to the party with the intention to fight and that the outcome had a lot to do with the fact that he was drunk. He was close to his family, especially his father who, like Ron, had been involved in serious assaults. Ron was taught to value and maintain his reputation for

fighting, which may explain his "tough" attitude and disrespect for authority expressed several times throughout the interview.

Tara (age 16)

Tara is Katie's older sister, and she was involved in the beating of the female youth. Tara picked up the victim, hit her once and walked away; she too was charged with aggravated assault. Tara had one other assault conviction. She did not think of herself as a violent person and, unlike her sister, did not view her life at home as a contributing factor in the crime. She admitted to alcohol being a major problem for her mom, whom she had seen in several fights. Tara previously had been a permanent ward of the state. During the interview she wanted to make it very clear that the incident was not in keeping with her personality. She was very articulate and knowledgeable about the system.

Todd (age 17)

Todd received a life sentence without eligibility for parole for the second-degree murder of a seventy-year-old man. Todd was also facing the possibility of being transferred to an adult prison when he turned eighteen. He and his co-accused had used drugs and were drunk the night of the incident. On their way home, the two stopped at a house for what Todd believed "was just going to be a B&E." His co-accused stabbed the man to death, but Todd was charged because he was there, he did not try to stop the murder and he did not report the crime. He blamed his co-accused but felt badly for what happened. He had a previous charge of assault. He was described by the OCP as a "pleasant kid," and he grew up in a very good home environment. During the interview he was calm and, at times, indifferent.

Appendix II

Summary of Establishment Authority Respondents

Seven of the respondents interviewed were from Youth Court Services (YCS) which is a government institution involved in assessing youths who are convicted under the Young Offenders Act (YOA).

Psychologists (2)
As part of the assessment process for YCS, psychologists were partially responsible for predisposition reports to give to the judges as an indication of the youths' fitness to stand trial; assessment of the offenders' needs, problems and appropriate sentences; and recommendations to raise cases to adult court for youths who commit serious crimes. The psychological assessment included intellectual, personality and projective testing. The youths were observed in both out-patient and in-patient departments. The psychologists administered treatment for sex offenders through individual counselling and group therapy in addition to conducting anger management session and other forms of one-to-one counselling.

Psychiatric Social Workers (3)
These authorities were involved in various forms of individual and group therapy. Psychiatric social workers were also part of the assessment, with the particular duty of providing the background or social history of the offender through speaking with people, such as parents, teachers and probation officers, who have the most contact with a youth. One of the psychiatric social workers had experience as an anger management specialist.

Psychiatrist
At YCS, the psychiatrist was involved in assessment, treatment, follow-up procedures and clinicals for sex offenders. He responded to the youths in Willingdon when they had problems, and he was responsible for prescribing medications. The psychiatrist had assessed the youths in twenty-five murder cases and could not recall one where the youth had not been drinking.

Clinical Director of Youth Court Services

The director had been planning to implement an expanded anger management program which incorporated violent group treatment. This was to entail a multi-system enterprise incorporating group therapy and family therapy (including group homes and probation). The director recognized the staff, financial and space restrictions in Willingdon and indicated that we needed to appeal to the youths' self-interest and business sense in terms of goals for the future.

Detective Constable, Vancouver City Police

The Constable was part of a team of ten constables and one supervisor in a specialized unit designed to deal both with youth violence issues in and around schools and with any problem away from the schools such as those occurring in "hang-outs." The constable was involved in lengthy investigations from the initial crime and charges to the follow-up in any offence involving youths. The police supported prevention through family, community and parental involvement in curbing violent youth crime.

Local Director of the "New" Youth Services Team (Burnaby)

The local director was referred to as a "team leader" and was responsible for the model, and eventual implementation, of youth services for the Ministry of Child and Family Services. The "team" included eighteen positions, which consisted of probation officers (one sex offender worker and four to deal with the Burnaby caseload); social workers; one resource person for office and administration duties in matters such as foster homes; two mental health workers; one drug and alcohol worker; and a special counsellor connected to the school system.

Officer in Charge of Programming (OCP)—Willingdon Detention Centre

The OCP helped me to arrange the interviews with the youths and obtained all the parental consent. It was the responsibility of the OCP to orient the youths once they were sentenced to Willingdon, to assess their needs, to determine their length of stay and to program the youths based on these variables. She had a lot of daily contact with the youths and worked with them to set goals and change detrimental behaviour.

Probation Officers (3)

All three probation officers had at some point been part of the Youth Specialized Probation Unit, which dealt with the most violent offenders and street youth through intensive supervision. One of the probation officers was acting supervisor of the unit; the second was in charge of ensuring continuity in probation services since the amalgamation of the ministries; and the third was an officer of the court, saw clients, networked with group homes, authorities of the court and various counsellors and wrote reports.

Youth Court Judges (2)

One of the youth court judges conducted a provincial inquiry into the services for children and youth and his recommendation led to the amalgamation of the five separate ministries into the newly created Ministry of Children and Family Services. An integration of services was believed to decrease the number of youths who "fall through the cracks." The judge indicated that the public was alarmed over the number of violent youth crimes for good reason, and he was trying to send out the message that all youths coming before him for Skytrain robberies are going to jail. The second judge made off-the-record comments during a telephone interview. He stated that self-esteem is a major issue for the youths and that there was a need to challenge the business community and marshall resources to get these kids a job upon their release.

References

Aber, J., and D. Cicchetti. 1984. "Socioemotional Development in Maltreated Children: An Empirical and Theoretical Analysis." In Fitzgerald, Lester and Yogman (eds.), *Theory and Research in Behavioural Paediatrics*, Volume 2. New York: Plenum.

Acland, Charles R. 1995. *Youth, Murder, Spectacle: The Cultural Politics of "Youth in Crisis."* San Francisco: Westview.

Adler, L. Loeb, and F. Denmark. 1995. *Violence and the Prevention of Violence.* Westport: Praeger.

American Psychological Association. 1993. *Violence and Youth: Psychology's Response.* Washington: American Psychological Association.

Ambert, A. 1986. "The Place of Children in North American Sociology." In P. Adler and P. Adler (eds.), *Sociological Studies in Child Development*. Connecticut: JAI.

Aries, P. 1962. *Centuries of Childhood.* Harmondsworth: Penguin.

Artz, S. 1998. *Sex, Power and the Violent School Girl*. Toronto: Trifolium.

Artz, S., and T. Riecken. 1994. "The Survey of Student Life." *A Study of Violence Among Adolescent Female Students in a Suburban School District*. Unpublished Report, British Columbia Ministry of Education, Education Research Unit.

Awad, G., E. Saunders, and J. Levene. 1984. "A Clinical Study of Male Adolescent Sexual Offenders." *International Journal of Offender Therapy and Comparative Criminology* 28(2):105–15.

Ayllan, T., and N. Azuin. 1968. *The Token Economy*. New York: Appleton Century.

Bagley, C., and D. Shewchuk-Dann. 1991. "Characteristics of 60 Children and Adolescents Who Have a History of Sexual Assault Against Others: Evidence from a Controlled Study." *Journal of Child and Youth Care* Special Issue:45–52.

Bala, N., R. Weiler, P. Copple, R.B. Smith, J.P. Hornick, and J.J. Paetsch. 1994. *A Police Reference Manual on Youth and Violence.* Ottawa: Canadian Research Institute for Law and the Family. Solicitor General Canada.

Barkley, Jacqueline. 1998. "The Politics of Parenting and the Youth Crisis." In Samuelson and Antony (eds.), *Power and Resistance: Critical Thinking about Canadian Social Issues*. Halifax: Fernwood.

Benedict, R. 1955. "Continuities and Discontinuities in Cultural Conditioning." In M. Mead and M. Wolfenstein (eds.), *Childhood in Contemporary Cultures*. Chicago: Chicago University Press.

Bergman, L. 1992. "Dating Violence Among High School Students." *Social Work* 37(1):21–27.

Boyden, J. 1990. "Childhood and the Policy Makers: A Comparative Perspective on the Globalization of Childhood." In Allison James and Alan Prout (eds.), *Constructing and Reconstructing Childhood: Contemporary Issues in the Sociological Study of Childhood*. London: Falmer.

Brunet, R. "'Justice Monkeys' with Baseball Bats: Beatings Cause Fears of Big-city-style Youth Gangs in the Okanagan." *British Columbia Report* 7(48):42–43.

Burchard, J., and P. Harig. 1976. "Behavior Modification and Juvenile Delinquency." In H. Leiternberg (ed.), *Handbook of Behavior Modification and Behavior*

Therapy. New Jersey: Prentice-Hall.

Cain, Maureen. 1990. "Towards Transgression: New Directions in Feminist Criminology." *International Journal of the Sociology of Law* 18:1–18.

Carrington, Peter J. 1995. "Has Violent Youth Crime Increased? Comment on Corrado and Markwart." *Canadian Journal of Criminology* 37(1):61–73.

Carrithers, M., S. Collins, and S. Lukes, eds. 1985. *The Category of the Person: Anthropology, Philosophy, History.* Cambridge: Cambridge University Press.

Centerwall, B. 1992. "Television and Violence." *Journal of the American Medical Association* 267:3059–63.

Chisholm, J. 1995. "Violent Youth: Reflections on Contemporary Child-rearing Practices in the United States as an Antecedent Cause." In L. Loeb Adler and F. Denmark (eds.), *Violence and the Prevention of Violence.* Westport: Praeger.

Cohen, Stanley. 1985. *Visions of Social Control.* Toronto: Polity.

_____. 1980. *Folk Devils and Moral Panics: The Creation of the Mods and Rockers.* Second edition. New York: St. Martin's.

Conrad, P., and J. Schneider. 1980. *Deviance and Medicalisation: From Badness to Sickness.* New York: C.V. Mosby.

Cornell, C., and R. Gelles. 1982. "Adolescent to Parent Violence." *Urban Social Change Review* 15(Winter):8–14.

Corrado, R., N. Bala, R. Linden, and M. Le Blanc. 1992. *Juvenile Justice in Canada: A Theoretical and Analytical Assessment.* Vancouver: Butterworths.

Corrado, R.R., and A. Markwart. 1994. "The Need to Reform the YOA in Response to Violent Young Offenders: Confusion, Reality or Myth?" *Canadian Journal of Criminology* 36(3):343–78.

Coupland, D. 1991. *Generation X: Tales for an Accelerated Culture.* New York: St. Martin's.

Cusson, M. 1990. "School Violence: The Problem and the Solution." *Apprentissage et Socialisation* 13:213–21.

Davis, M. 1988. "Los Angeles: Civil Liberties between the Hammer and the Rock." *New Left Review* 170(July–August):37–60.

Davison, G., and J. Neale. 1994. *Abnormal Psychology.* Sixth edition. Toronto: John Wiley.

DeKeseredy, W., and K. Kelly. 1993. "Incidence and Prevalence of Wife Abuse in Canadian University and College Dating Relationships." *Canadian Journal of Sociology* 18: 137–59.

Department of Justice. 1999. *Canada's Youth Criminal Justice Act: A New Law—A New Approach.* http://canada.justice.gc.ca/en/dept/pub/ycja/youth/htm.

Doob, A, V. Marinos, and K. Varma. 1995. *Youth Crime and the Youth Justice System in Canada: A Research Perspective.* Toronto: Centre of Criminology, University of Toronto.

Edelman, M. 1977. *Political Language: Words That Succeed and Policies That Fail.* New York: Academic.

Ellis, D., and W. DeKeseredy. 1994. *Pre-test Report on the Frequency, Severity and Patterning of Sibling Violence in Canadian Families: Causes and Consequences.* Ottawa: Health Canada, Family Violence Prevention Division.

Ennew, E. 1986. *The Sexual Exploitation of Children.* Cambridge: Polity.

Fairholm, J. 1993. *Dating Violence Prevention: Overview and Response.* Vancouver: Canadian Red Cross.

References

Finch, J. 1985. *Research and Policy: Uses of Qualitative Methods in Social and Educational Research*. Lewes: Falmer.

Funckenauer, J.O. 1982. *Scared Straight! And the Panacea Phenomenon*. Englewood Cliffs, NJ: Prentice-Hall.

Finkelhor, D., and J. Dziuba-Leatherman. 1994. "Victimization of Children." *American Psychologist* 49:173–83.

Fitzpatrick, D., and C. Halliday. 1992. *Not the Way to Love: Violence Against Young Women in Dating Relationships*. Amherst, N.S.: Cumberland County Transition House.

Foley, W. 1974. *A Child in the Forest*. London: BBC.

Foucault, M. 1980. *Michel Foucault: Power and Knowledge*. London: Harvester Wheatsheaf.

_____. 1979. *Discipline and Punish: The Birth of the Prison*. New York: Vintage.

Frank, J. 1992. "Violent Youth Crime." *Canadian Social Trends* Autumn:2–8.

Gamble, R. 1979. *Chelsea Childhood*. London: BBC.

Garland, D. 1990. *Punishment and Modern Society: A Study in Social Theory*. Chicago: University of Chicago Press.

_____. 1985. *Punishment and Welfare: A History of Penal Strategies*. Aldershot U.K.: Gower.

Gelber, S. 1990. The Juvenile Justice System: Vision for the Future. *Juvenile and Family Court Journal* 41:5–18.

Giddens, A. 1990. *The Consequences of Modernity*. Cambridge: Polity.

Giroux, H. 1996. *Fugitive Cultures: Race, Violence and Youth*. New York: Routledge.

Green, A. 1985. "Generational Transmission of Violence in Child Abuse." *International Journal of Family Psychiatry* 6(4):389–403.

Greenspan, E.L. 1994. *Martin's Annual Criminal Code 1994*. Ontario: Law Book.

Haapanen, R. 1991. *Patterns of Violent Crime: A Longitudinal Investigation*. Sacramento: State of California, Department of the Youth Authority, Research Division.

Haines, K. 1996. *Understanding Modern Juvenile Justice: The Organisational Context of Service Provision*. England: Avebury.

Hall, S., C. Critcher, T. Jefferson, J. Clarke, J., and B. Roberts. 1978. *Policing the Crisis: Mugging, the State and Law and Order*. London: Macmillan.

Hardman, C. 1973. "Can There Be an Anthropology of Children?" *Journal of Anthropology Society of Oxford* 4(1):85–99.

Hare, R. 1993. *Without Conscience: The Disturbing World of the Psychopaths Among Us*. New York: Pocket.

Harris, R., and D. Webb. 1987. *Welfare, Power, and Juvenile Justice: The Social Control of Delinquent Youth*. London: Tavistock.

Hepworth, M., and B. Turner. 1982. *Confession: Studies in Deviance and Religion*. Boston: Routledge and Kegan Paul.

Herman, J., B. Mowder, L. Moy, and L. Sadler. 1995. "Trauma in Children's Lives: Issues and Treatment." In Adler and Denmark (eds.), *Violence and the Prevention of Violence*. Westport: Praeger.

Hockey, J., and A. James. 1993. *Growing Up and Growing Old: Ageing and Dependency in the Life Course*. London: Sage.

Hornick, J., F. Bolitho, and D. LeClaire. 1994. *Young Offenders and the Sexual Abuse of Children*. Ottawa: Department of Justice.

Hotaling, G.T., M.A. Staus, and A.J. Lincoln. 1989. In L. Ohlin and M. Tornry (eds.), *Family Violence*. Chicago: University of Chicago Press. 315–75.

Howell, J., B. Krisberg, and M. Jones. 1995. "Trends in Juvenile Crime and Youth Violence." In J. Howell, B. Krisberg, J.D. Hawking and J.J. Wilson (eds.), *Serious, Violent and Chronic Juvenile Offenders*. Thousand Oaks: Sage.

James, Allison. 1993. *Childhood Identities: Self and Social Relationships in the Experience of the Child*. Edinburgh: Edinburgh University Press.

James, Allison, and Chris Jenks. 1996. "Public Perceptions of Childhood Criminality." *British Journal of Sociology* 47(2):315–30.

James, Allison, and Alan Prout, eds. 1990. *Constructing and Reconstructing Childhood: Contemporary Issues in the Sociological Study of Childhood*. London: Falmer.

Jenks, C., ed. 1982. *The Sociology of Childhood*. London: Batsford.

Katz, J. 1988. *Seductions of Crime: Moral and Sensual Attractions of Doing Evil*. New York: Basic.

Kelly, B. 1992. *Children Inside: Rhetoric and Practice in a Locked Institution for Children*. London: Routledge.

Kingsley, B. 1994. *Common Assault in Canada*. Ottawa: Canadian Centre for Justice Statistics.

Kohlberg, L. 1969. "Stage and Sequence: The Cognitive Developmental Approach to Socialization." In D. Goslin (ed.), *Handbook of Socialization Theory and Research*. Chicago: Rand.

Kruttschnitt, C., and M. Dornfeld. 1991. "Childhood Victimization, Race and Violent Crime." *Criminal Justice and Behaviour* 18:448–63.

Lattimore, Pamela K., C. Visher, and R. Linster. 1995. "Predicting Rearrest for Violence Among Serious Youthful Offenders." *Journal of Research in Crime and Delinquency* 32(1):54–83.

Lefer, L. 1984. "The Fine Edge of Violence." *Journal of the American Academy of Psychoanalysis* 12(2):253–68.

Leonard, T. 1993. "Highlights 1992–93." *Juristat Service Bulletin* 13(5):1–15.

Lewis, D.O., C. Mallouh, and V. Webb. 1989. "Child Abuse, Delinquency and Violent Criminality." In C. Cicchetti and V. Carlson (ed.), *Child Maltreatment*. New York: Cambridge University Press.

Lilly, Robert J., Francis T. Cullen, and Richard A. Ball. 1995. *Criminological Theory: Context and Consequences*. Second Edition. Thousand Oaks: Sage.

Lipsey, M. 1992. "Juvenile Delinquency Treatment: A Meta-analytic Inquiry into the Variability of Effects." In T.D. Cook, H. Cooper, D.S. Cordray, H. Harmann, L.V. Hedges, R.J. Kight, T.A. Louis and F. Mosteller (eds.), *Meta-analysis for Explanation*. New York: Russell Sage.

MacDougall, J. 1993. *Violence in the Schools: Programs and Policies for Prevention*. Toronto: Canadian Education Association.

MacKay, R. 1973. "Conceptions of Children and Models of Socialization." In Hans Peter Dreitzel (ed.), *Childhood and Socialization*. London: Macmillan.

May, R. 1972. *Power and Innocence: A Search for the Sources of Violence*. New York: Norton.

Mead, M. 1928. *Coming of Age in Samoa*. Middlesex: Penguin.

Merlo, J. 1995. "Juvenile Violence and the Death Penalty." In L. Loeb Adler and F. Denmark (eds.), *Violence and the Prevention of Violence*. Westport: Praeger.

References

Miller, Jerome. 1991. *Last One Over the Wall: The Massachusetts Experiment in Closing Reform Schools*. Columbus: Ohio State University Press.

Milne, H., R. Linden, and R. Kueneman. 1992. "Advocate or Guardian: The Role of Defence Counsel in Youth Justice." In R. Corrado, N. Bala, R. Linden, and M. LeBlanc (eds.), *Juvenile Justice in Canada: A Theoretical and Analytical Assessment*. Vancouver: Butterworths.

Nasty Girls. 1997. Canadian Broadcasting Corporation. March 5. Producer Maureen Palmer. Reporter Margo Harper.

National Clearinghouse on Family Violence. 1993. *National Inventory of Treatment Programs for Child Sexual Abuse Offenders*. Ottawa: Health Canada.

New York Times. 1992. "Mowing down our children." Editorial. Vol. 142. November 9:A16.

O'Donoghue, J. 1995. "Violence in the Schools." In L. Loeb Adler and F. Denmark (eds.), *Violence and the Prevention of Violence*. Westport: Praeger.

Palys, T. 1995. *Research Decisions: Qualitative and Quantitative Perspectives*. Second edition. Toronto: Harcourt.

Palys, Ted, and John Lowman. 1998. *Memorandum to the Ethics Committee from Dr. Palys and Dr. Lowman*. February 3. Burnaby, B.C.: Simon Fraser University.

Pearson, P. 1997. *When She Was Bad: Violent Women and the Myth of Innocence*. New York: Viking Penguin.

Phaneuf, G. 1990. *Dating Violence*. Ottawa: Health Canada, National Clearinghouse on Family Violence.

Pierce, L., and R. Pierce. 1987. "Incestuous Victimization by Juvenile Sex Offenders." *Journal of Family Violence* 2(4):351–64.

Public Health Service, U.S. Department of Health and Human Services. 1991. *Healthy People 2000: National Health Promotion and Disease Prevention Objectives*. Washington, D.C.: Government Printing Office.

Pynoos, R.S., and K. Nader. 1990. "Children's Exposure to Violence and Traumatic Death." *Psychiatric Annals* 20:334–44.

Qvortrup, J. 1990. "A Voice for Children in Statistical and Social Accounting: A Plea for Children's Rights to be Heard." In Allison James and Alan Prout (eds.), *Constructing and Reconstructing Childhood: Contemporary Issues in the Sociological Study of Childhood*. London: Falmer.

Roberts, J. 1995. "Sexual Assault Is a Crime of Violence." *Canadian Journal of Criminology* 37(1):88–95.

Saskatoon Star Phoenix. (1997). "Decision-making critical to youth: Child advocate." April 10: A3.

Saltzman, L.E., J.A. Mercy, P.W. O'Carroll, M. Rosenberg, and P.H. Thodes. 1992. "Weapon Involvement and Injury Outcomes in Family and Intimate Assaults." *New England Journal of Medicine* 322:3043–47.

Schissel, B. 1997. *Blaming Children: Youth Crime, Moral Panics and the Politics of Hate*. Halifax: Fernwood.

_____. 1993. *The Social Dimensions of Canadian Youth Justice*. Don Mills, Ontario: Oxford University Press.

Sloan, J.H., F.P. Rivara, A.T. Reay, J.A. Ferris, and A.L. Kellerman. 1990. "Firearm Regulations and Rates of Suicide: A Comparison of Two Metropolitan Areas." *New England Journal of Medicine* 322:369–73.

Smith, C.A., and T.P. Thornberry. 1993. *The Relationship Between Childhood Mal-

treatment and Adolescent Involvement in Delinquency and Drug Use. Paper presented at the annual meeting of the Society for Research on Child Development, New Orleans.

Smith, Dorothy E. 1992. "Sociology from Women's Experience: A Reaffirmation." *Sociological Theory* 10(1):88–98.

_____. 1987. *The Everyday World as Problematic: A Feminist Sociology.* Boston: Northeaster University Press.

Smith, R. 1993. *Psychology.* Minneapolis: West.

Snyder, H., and M. Sickmund. 1995. *Juvenile Offenders and Victims: A National Report.* Washington: Office of Juvenile Justice and Delinquency Prevention.

Stallybrass, P., and A. White. 1986. *The Politics and Poetics of Transgression.* Ithaca: Cornell University Press.

Statistics Canada, Canadian Centre for Justice Statistics. 1994. *Canadian Crime Statistics 1992.* Ottawa: Statistics Canada.

Stuart, D. 1993. "Sexual Assault: Substantive Issues Before and After Bill C-49." *Criminal Law Quarterly* 35(2):241–63.

Sugarman, D., and G. Hotaling. 1991. "Dating Violence: A Review of Contextual and Risk Factors." In B. Levy (ed.), *Dating Violence: Young Women in Danger.* Seattle: Seal.

U.S. Congress, Office of Technology Assessment. 1991. Adolescent Health: Background and the Effectiveness of Selected Prevention and Treatment Services. Vol. 2. November. Washington, D.C.: Government Printing Office.

Vancouver Sun. 1997a. "Charging children young as 10 recommended in MPs' study." April 19:A4.

Vancouver Sun. 1997b. "Violent youth, crime victims top Justice Minister's agenda." August 23:A1.

Vancouver Sun. 1997c. "The net generation gets ready to download society." November 8:E19.

Walker, S.G. 1993. *Salient Issues from Focus Groups, Interviews and Documentation from Police, Educators and Customs Personnel: Weapons Use in Schools/Border Crossings by Canadian Youth.* Unpublished paper. Ottawa: Solicitor General.

Weiler, R., T. Caputo, and K. Kelly. 1993. *Reports in Selected Canadian Newspapers and Magazines on Youth Violence and Youth Gangs.* Unpublished paper. Ottawa: Solicitor General.

Weiler, R., and Associates Ltd. 1994. *Collective Youth Violence and Youth Gangs: A Summary of Interview and Site Visits in Selected Canadian Communities.* Unpublished paper. Ottawa: Solicitor General.

Western Report. 1996. "A Lull before the Teenage Storm: Teen Violence Stats are Up and More Crime is on the Way." 11(31):12.

Widom, C.S. 1992. *The Cycle of Violence.* Washington, D.C.: U.S. Department of Justice, National Institute of Justice.

Willis, P. 1977. *Learning to Labour: How Working Class Kids Get Working Class Jobs.* New York: Columbia University Press.

Wolman, B. 1995. "Foreword."0 In Adler and Denmark (eds.), *Violence and the Prevention of Violence.* Westport: Praeger.

Wright-Mills, C. 1959. *The Sociological Imagination.* New York: Oxford University Press.

Yule, W. 1977. "Behavioural Approaches." In M. Rutter and L. Hersov (eds.), *Child Psychology: Modern Approache*s. Oxford: Blackwell.

Index